MW01644477

Chamudei Shai on the Torah and Holidays

Eternal Wisdom

Faith & Resilience: Our Jewish story–past, present and future

Table Of Contents

Letters of Praise and Approbation....................4

Introduction from the original Hebrew edition....16

Introduction to this volume 21

Yom Kippur...24

Succos and Shemini Atzeres................................44

Parashas Bereishis 57

Parashas Lech Lecha 71

Parashas Vayeira..82

Parashas Chayei Sarah 101

Parashas Toldos 108

Parashas Vayeitzei...128

Parashas Vayishlach 149

Parashas Mikeitz-Chanukah..............................189

Parashas Vayigash..204

Parashas Vayechi 216

In Conclusion and in Celebration 231

A Brief Biographical Sketch of the Chavos Yair ...237

Letters of Praise and Approbation

BS"D (With the Help of G-d)

Hanukkah, 5784

Honorable and dear friend, the gaon Rabbi Shlomo [Shvartz], may he be well,

I wish to express my gratitude to you for the delightful and charming book by Rabbi Geliebter, may he be well. I cannot contain my excitement, although we already discussed it just last week. Thank G-d, every day I hear more and more people who have studied the sefer and greatly enjoyed it.

There is something very interesting that many people mention—it is unique and intriguing, not something they are accustomed to seeing, such a profound and insightful interpretation. I wholeheartedly agree because it combines a significant part of his innovations that delve deep. It is fascinating to see how it integrates into both verses and the explanations of earlier and later scholars. It is a valuable asset to the Jewish people—both the profound explanation and the simplification for the reader. Everyone, on their own level, finds it special and experiences pure enjoyment in reading.

I kindly ask you to convey this to the author of Chamudei Shai—I don't even know if he is aware of the special quality that his wonderful book

I presented all of these teachings in the name of *Chamudei Shai*.

At the end of the prayers, a number of people came up to me and told me, "We have been listening to you speak for a number of years, but we have never heard such wonderful, sweet and lovely ideas." I acknowledged to them that these ideas aren't mine, but those of my friend, R. Shlomo Yosef.

Then, as my family was in the middle of our meal, a member of the congregation came to our door and requested a copy of *Machmadei HaTorah*, which I gave to him. The next day he told me, "We learned *Chamudei Shai* at our table and it fortified our faith in Hashem."

And I look forward to see the joy of the holiday, to see how Hashem's word bolsters the people of Israel.

Fortunate are you, R. Shlomo Yosef. The words of your Torah sparkle and give joy to G-d and man.

With all good wishes, from your friend who loves you,

Shlomo Shvartz
28 Nissan 5780

ביהמ"ד גבול יעבץ
ברוקלין, נוא יארק

דוד קאהן

מכתב ברכה

בא לפני ידידי שהנני מכיר אותו רבות בשנים,
הרב שלמה יוסף גולדבערג שליט"א, והראה לי קטעים מספר
שחיבר על שזכה להגיע לשבעים שנה (עיין שו"ת חות
יאיר סימן ע' שהורה שנכון לברך ברכת שהחינו כשהאדם
מגיע לגיל זה)

והנני משתתף בשמחתו, וגם במה שחוגג מאורע
זה לחבר דברי תורה. כמה יפה פעולה זו לחבר
שמחת חיים עם שמחת תורה. ברכתי מקרב לב שיצליח
בכל דרכיו וישמח במעשיו

החותם בהוקרה וכ"ת
דוד קאהן
ח' טבת תשפ"ג

All letters of approbation were originally included in the Hebrew edition of this volume.
חמודי שי על התורה והמועדים חלק ראשון: **בראשית** מועדי ירח האיתנים חנוכה

בס"ד

שמואל קמנצקי
Rabbi S. Kamenetsky

2018 Upland Way
Philadelphia, PA 19131

Home: 215-473-2798
Study: 215-473-1212

[illegible]

[illegible]

[illegible]

[illegible]

[illegible]

[illegible]

[illegible]

[illegible]

[illegible]

[illegible]

[illegible]

[illegible]

שמואל קמנצקי

בס"ד

הרב שלמה שוורץ

רב בשכונת קטמון

יו"ר מערכת מחמדי התורה

עיה"ק ירושלים תובב"א

אור ליום ו' ערש"ק פר' תצוה - זכור תשפ"ג

מה תרב שמחתי בראותי את פרי היצירה הנפלאה ספר חמודי שי, דברים מחוכמים, ישרים ונפלאים, מאירים כספירים, רואיו יאמרו ברקאי, קוראיו יתעלו ויתענגו, מעשיו ידיו להתפאר, של האי גברא רבא ויקירא, אוהב תורה בצורה נפלאה ומיוחדת שאין הנמצא כמוהו, כל דבר חידוש נאמרת ברמ"ח איברים ושס"ה גידים, ופניו בוערות כלפידים, חשקת תורה לאין ערוך, בבהירות כשולחן הערוך.

ה"ה ידידי היקר למאוד, מסולא בפז ויקר והוד, אוהב ורודף חסד וצדקות, משכיל אל דל ומקשיב לזעקות

הרבני החסיד רבי **שלמה יוסף געליבטער** שליט"א

לורענץ נויא יורק

אשריך שעלית ונתעלית למאוד, וחפץ נפשך הוצאת כיסוד, יעלה זכרוני כל הימים, כאשר לפעמים, חידושים ארכו לילות שלמים, העמדת נקודות אשר עין לא ראתה, לחדש בכל עת וזמן נעלית, נדברנו יחדיו בתורת ה' להגות, חידושים ומוסר ודברי הגות, ועלו על מזבח הדפוס, דבר שבוע בשבוע לי הזכות, פיאר את גליוננו מחמדי התורה, אשר לו היה כשער אורה, יושבי על מדין רבנן ותלמידיהון, ציפו לחידושים אלו בכליון, ואמרו איה הגליון, להתענג בטעם העליון.

ובפרט לעת עתה, כאשר לשנת השבעים הגעת, את פרי עמל לאור עולם הוצאת, וכולם משבחים ואומרים אתה יצרת, כליל תפארת בראשו נתת, על חנוכה ירח האיתנים לראשונה הצבת, בראשית לזאת הודעת, כל זאת ערכת וכתבת.

ברכתי לידידי הנערץ, לעולם תנשא ותוערץ, יהא ה' בעזרך בכל דרכיך, טוב וחסד ורחמים בכל שעריך, בבריאות השלימה כל ימי חייך, אתה ובניך ובני בניך, וכל משפחתך הרוממה, עדי נזכה לגאולה השלימה

מברך בברכת התורה ולומדיה

שלמה שוורץ

Bais Medrash of Harborview
218 Harborview South
Lawrence, New York 11559

Rabbi Yehoshua Kalish

לכ' ידידי היקר ר' יוסי,

שמחתי מאוד לראות דבריך הנחמדים והנעימים על הימים לפני [illegible]
דרשות התשובה. בן יכבד אב. ובכבוד הני אקוה [illegible]. והמאוד שי
יהיה לנחת ולתפארת נשמת לאביך [illegible] ובבית [illegible] והמבואר שבנית אם
נוות ביתך שתחי' [illegible] על דוממות מדותיך ונראות [illegible] שקדמה לחכמתך.
ואמתך לבי אני מברך אותך שתמשיך ללמוד וללמד ולחדש חידושים נפלאים
לזכות הרבה מתוך משפחתך היקרה.

חברך אוהבך מאוד
יהושע

בס"ד

CONGREGATION KNESETH ISRAEL

728 Empire Avenue
Far Rockaway, NY 11691

Phone: 718.327.0500
Fax: 718.327.7415

www.whiteshul.com
office@whiteshul.com

Rabbi
Rabbi Eytan Feiner

Associate Rabbi
Rabbi Motti Neuburger

Rabbi Emeritus
Rabbi Ralph Pelcovitz זצ"ל

President
Ely Pasternak

Co-Chairmen of the Board
Nesanel Feller
Tuvia Silverstein

Vice-Presidents
Adam Kay
Barry Salamon
Aryeh Satt
Yehuda Yovits

Vice-Chairman of the Board
Matisyahu Hedvat

Treasurer
Shimmy Berger

Gabbai
Mattie Schwartz

מוצש"ק פר' בא, ו' שבט תשע"ט לפ"ק

מכתב ברכה

אחר שמחתי ונהניתי לראות ולעיין מספרו הנפלא
של ידידי ויקירי הרב שלמה יוסף גולדשטיין שליט"א
אשר הפליא לעשות ברוב עומק לחבר חידושים על הגמרא
ועל המועדים, דברים מתוקים וערבים המשמחים על הלב טוב
טעם ודעת.

יישר חילך לאורייתא, והמקום אשר עזרך עד הלום יעזרך
ויתן בלבך ברכה והצלחה ותזכה לראות ברכה בכל מעשיך
ובכל מעשי ידיך, ויהא שמעתיך לזכות הרבים מתורתך הרחבה.
בעזה"י, תמשיך ללמוד וללמד להגדיל תורה ולהאדירה מתוך
בריאות גופא ונהורא מעליא יחד עם רעייתך היקרה שתחי', ותזכו
לאריכות ימים ושנים טובים רב נחת ושמחה תמיד. אמן

יה"ר שחיבורו המחובר שהוציא לאור כבר תמיד יהי לרצון
לפני האלוקים והחשוב יהיה לנחת רוח לכל בני המשפחה השלמה,
ותגבה נשמתו הטהורה לעלות מחיל אל חיל בגן עדן עולה,
עד ביאת גו"צ ותחיית המתים בב"א.

הכותב ומחכה לכבוד המחבר הנעלה,
ידידו מוקירו מאד ומברכו בכל לב,

איתן דוד פיינר

Member of ORTHODOX UNION
Enhancing Jewish Life

אמת ומשפט שלום שפטו בשעריכם

הרב יוסף יצחק אדרעי
מחבר ספר
"מטבח כהלכה"

בס"ד

יום שלישי י"ג אייר תשפ"ד

הגדתי היום בשבח הספרים החשובים

חמודי שי

שחיברם הרה"ג הרה"ח שלמה יוסף געליבטער יצ"ו עוסק בצורכי ציבור באמונה ועוזר ומסייע לחיילי צה"ל העומדים על משמר ארצנו וערי אלוקינו בגופו ובממנו ועליו אמרו חז"ל הקב"ה ישלם שכרו אמן,

בן הרב החסיד יהודה אריה לייב געליבעטער זצ"ל אוד מוצל מאש אשר עבר את כול מדורי הגהנום בשנות הזעם זכה להקים את משפחתו לזכר כול הקדושים השם ינקום דמם זצ"ל

הרבה עמל ויגיעה השקיע המחבר בספריו כדי לחזק את עם ישראל,

והקב"ה חנן אתו בשכל ישר, והלומד מן הספר יתעורר ליראת השם,

וכבר אמרו חז"ל "אמר רבי חלבו אמר רב הונא, כל שיש בו יראת שמים דבריו נשמעים, שנאמר "סוף דבר הכל נשמע את אלקים ירא ואת מצוותיו שמור כי זה כל האדם" (ברכות ו' ע"ב).

והרב הנ"ל ירא השם מרבים ודבריו יוצאים מליבו הטהור ונכנסים לליבות של עם ישראל לחזקם לתורה וליראת השם,

ובזכות זה נזכה לראות בנחמת ציון וירושלים בב"א

החותם בברכה כאן עיר הקודש ירושלים

הרב אדרעי יוסף יצחק

הרב יוסף יצחק אדרעי
רב ומו"צ
עה"ק ירושלים

ת.ד. 39226 מיקוד 9139102 הר נוף ירושלים
0528203284 02-6529032

יצחק דוד אלטר

רחוב ר' יהודה הלוי 15 בני ברק

בה"י, ער"ח אד' תשע"ח

הן הובאו לפני ספר חמודי ש' מהרבני ה"ח שלמה יוסף געלדבערג שי' לאוי"ט
שם העלה פנינים והארות שחננו השי"ת בתורה, ועתה עלתה ברצונו
לשוב לחדש במהדורא תנינא בהוספת שבח, ואמינא לפעלא טבא
אישר, וברכתי שעוד ינובון בשיבה דשנים ורעננים יהיו
לעשות ספרים ולפרחים בתורת ד'. מתוך בריות גופא
ולהפיץ ממעינותיו לשלח על פני חוצות.

ובאתי עה"ח ביקרא דאורייתא

יצחק דוד אלטר
ראש בית התלמוד להוראה-גור ב"ב

ישראל פאנעט
נו"נ להגה"ק בעל המראה יחזקאל" זי"ע
מקארלסבורג
יואל 17 בני ברק 03-5795962

Rabbi Israel Panet
from Carlsburg
17 Yoel St. Bnei Brak, Israel
+972-35795962

בס"ד

י"ג סיון תשפ"ד פעיה"ת בני ברק

לכבוד ידידי הגאון המופלא רבי **שלמה יוסף** שליט"א

כעת אני יושב בביתי בבני ברק, ומתוך ישוב הדעת אני יכול לכתוב לך, כי הספר **חמודי שי** לא מש מעל שולחני, והיה לי עונג יום טוב רוחני וגשמי בחג השבועות העעל"ט, ושיתפתי ברעיונתיך את בני משפחתי כמובן בשם אומרם.

על פי בקשתך שגם אני אכתוב לך מרעיונתי, אכתוב לך בס"ד מה שהתחדש לי בעת התבוננותי בספרך, בבחינת דברי תורה פרין ורבין.

בספר חמודי שי בפרשת צו עמוד 59 מאריך מע"כ שליט"א בענין ההכנעה בשעת ההודאה וברכת מודים. חשבתי על פי זה, שחטא אדה"ר ע"י הנחש היה שאמר האשה אשר נתת עמדי וברש"י שם כ' כאן כפר הטובה והיינו שע"י הנחש הגיע לכפיות טובה, היפוך עניין ההודאה והכרת הטוב, ואולי לכן הגמרא בב"ק אומרת שמי שלא כורע במודים שדרתו הופכת לנחש, כי זה ענין אחד כפי שכתבת בספר שצריך להכניע את עצמו בהודאה ההפך ממידת הנחש.

ואולי לזה רמזו חז"ל במסכת יומא, וכי נחש ממית או נחש מחיה, אלא כל זמן שמביטין כלפי מעלה ומשעבדין ליבם לאביהם שבשמים היו מתרפאים. כי זה המטרה לתקן חטא הנחש להכנע ולהודות להשי"ת.

עוד ראיתי בספר בעמוד 96 בשם הוריו ז"ל "טראכט גוט וועט זיין גוט" ומאריך שם בענין קבלת יסורים מתוך שמחה ושירה. ראיתי בשפ"א בפרשת ראה, שאומר על דברי הירושלמי במגילה "מפני מה אמרו חכמים אין מפסיקין בקללות אמר הקב"ה אינו בדין שיהיו בני מתקללין ואני מתברך", ומחדש שם שאם אדם מקבל יסורים וזמנים קשים ומשבח בזה להקב"ה, אזי הקב"ה מעביר ממנו את היסורים, כי אינו בדין שיהיו בני מתקללין ואני מתברך.

וכן שמעתי מאבי שליט"א שאמר בשם האמרי אמת על הפסוק וידום אהרן, ועל הפסוק והמשכיל בעת ההיא ידום, שידום יש לו ב' פירושים, א'. לשתוק. ב'. מלשון דם, ואמר שאפילו כשירד ח"ו דם צריך לשתוק ולהודות להשי"ת. ודפח"ח.

ושוב הנני מודה למע"כ על הספר הנפלא ובכלל על עצם הזכות להכיר אדם יקר וחשוב כמע"כ, כי מתוך הספר רואים איך שזור בו מידותיך הנפלאים, שהכל בעניין מידות טובות והתבוננות טוב על כל הבריאה והנבראים, ואפשר לומר עליך הסופר והספר ירדו כרוכים מן השמים .

פשוט קיימתי בחג הזה מאמר חז"ל בשבת הכל מודים בעצרת דבעינן נמי לכם. כי העיון בספרך היה עונג גשמי ותענוג רוחני כאחד.

בידידות

בברכת יפוצו מעינתיך חוצה

ישראל פאנעט

בע"ה

Introduction from the original Hebrew edition

I will begin by praising and thanking Hashem for all of His good and His miracles with us every day, and for having given us life, maintained us, and brought us to this time.

I wrote *Chamudei Shai* principally due to the inspiration of my father, Rabbi Yehudah Aryeh Leib, the son of R. Moshe Mordechai, zatzal Geliebter, who passed away on 3 Cheshvan 5734 (1973). He was a Gerrer Chasid from Plotzk, Poland, who at a young age received rabbinic ordination from the leading rabbis of Poland. His rabbinic background was the determinative factor in his life, and helped him endure with utter self-sacrifice the hardest times in the course of the Shoah, which left him as the only survivor of his family—"a brand plucked from the fire." From the moment that he was liberated from the Buchenwald concentration camp, his mission in life was to help rehabilitate Jewish life for the sake of Hashem and His Torah, and for the sake of the people of Israel. He served in the rabbinate and was a *dayan* in the *beis din* in the displaced persons camp in Frankfurt-Zeilsheim and *av beis din* of the community of Offenbach until he came to the United States. He was one of the founders of the community of Gur Hasidim in Manhattan, and he gave weekly talks on the *Sefas Emes* and a *daf yomi* class. He also published a number of his *chiddushim* on the Torah and on prayer in rabbinic periodicals. Sadly, he did not attain "the days of our years are seventy years" (*Tehillim* 90:10). May this book be a monument for his pure soul.

This book began as a weekly *parashah* column in the Shabbos periodical published in Israel, *Machmadei HaTorah*, which features, in the words of the editor, "ideas on the *parashah* seasoned with words of our early and later rabbis."

It was not easy to produce these essays in keeping with the pace of the very tight weekly schedule, but with the help of heaven I wrote on the majority of the *parshiyos*.

A few months prior to reaching my seventieth birthday, I decided, with thanks for the past and prayer for the future, to review the material that had already been published and to revise the material and add additional *chiddushim* with more sources. I decided that I would celebrate my attainment of the age of seventy by completing all of the essays on *Sefer Bereishis* and on the holidays that occur in the course of the reading of *Sefer Bereishis* (and a little before it).

And with this, I present to my family and to the community of Torah learners the first volume of *Chamudei Shai* on *Sefer Bereishis* and on the Days of Awe, Succos, and Chanukah.

In Appreciation and Gratitude

First and foremost, I must praise and thank Hashem, the Master of all, for blessing me with my beloved wife Feigy (Feiga Yuta) שתחי׳ my partner in life, who has been my right hand in all that I have achieved.

Our prayer to Hashem is that we may attain length of days and years together with a healthy body and tranquil soul. And may we continue to see much *yiddishe nachas* from all of our offspring.

And I acknowledge and thank all of my teachers and rabbis, among them great Torah sages outstanding in their generation, such as the gaon Rabbi Mendel Kaplan zatzal, the gaon Rabbi Moshe Dovber Rivkin zatzal, and the gaon Rabbi Gedaliah Halevi Schorr zatzal.

And I acknowledge and thank my teacher and rabbi, the gaon R. Dovid Cohen shlita, rabbi of Gvul Ya'avetz in Brooklyn, NY, who is one of the great *poskim* in our generation.

I have benefited so much in being his student for more than thirty years and in learning Maharal on the Torah and other significant *seforim* together with him, in addition to drinking from the wellspring of his wisdom in all areas of the Torah together with his loving dedication to every Jew. I bless him with "the blessing of a simple person" for length of days and years with health and strength to continue his holy mission to serve the people of Israel, as he is filled with *nachas* from his beautiful family and from all of his offspring.

And last and most beloved, I acknowledge and thank the G-d-fearing and wise woman of valor, my mother and teacher, Mrs. Beila Liba Geliebter, of blessed memory, the daughter of R. Avraham Manis, who passed away on 13 Nissan 5771 (2011). I must honor my beloved mother, of blessed memory, who acted with valor during the Shoah and taught me every important lesson that I learned in life.

My thanks to the gaon Rabbi Shlomo Shvartz, shlita, editor of *Machmadei HaTorah* on the weekly *parashah,* in which the first edition of these essays was published in my weekly column, *Chamudei Shai,* who helped with the editing, and to my friend the gaon Rabbi Yochanan Bechhofer, shlita. They helped me edit the essays that had been previously published. May their reward from Hashem be complete.

"I am humbled by all of the kindnesses and by all of the truth" (*Bereishis* 32:11).

Shlomo Yosef Geliebter
25 Teves 5783

בע"ה

Introduction to this volume

The introduction to the original Hebrew edition focused on the celebration of writing my first Sefer, in commemoration of my 70th birthday. So much has happened since then.

The Hebrew edition of *Chamudei Shai* on *Bereishis* was published nearly two years ago for this special milestone in my life. Birthdays are viewed as times for reflection, for offering thanksgiving to Hashem for all His blessings, and as an opportunity for renewal and reinvigoration. Writing this *Sefer* on *Bereishis* to celebrate life ignited in me a desire to continue this important work. After completing *Chamudei Shai* on *Sefer Bereishis,* work proceeded immediately on *Shemos* and *Vayikra,* and both volumes were subsequently published.

This English edition is being released in the month of Elul, right before the High Holidays and when we get ready to start over. We are about to complete the yearly Torah reading and begin a new cycle from *Bereishis,* which follows the sequence of the *parshiyos* and holidays in this book.

Unfortunately, at the point of the recent completion of the Torah cycle, the attacks of Simchas Torah 5784 occurred and we were at war once again. In a time so desperately in need of strength and inspiration, my colleagues suggested that we produce a special pamphlet called *Chizukei Shai* on topics of Faith, Unity, and Prayer which were mostly culled from essays in this book. *Chizukei Shai* was then distributed to units of the Israel Defense Forces (IDF) and was well received. Similarly, a special *Chamudei Shai* Haggadah and a special Three Weeks Reader, *Nechamos Shai*, were produced to raise morale in the IDF.

Completing this English edition, as the war continues with no end in sight, has been a challenging endeavor. I am confident, however, that the readers of this book will, in the near future, reflect on this trying period as a continued part of the history of the Jewish people and how we always persevere despite hardship. My hope is to offer support and provide words of encouragement to endure and persevere. The essay "Reflections Post Simchas Torah 5784" in the Sukkos - Simchas Torah chapter develops this theme.

As mentioned throughout the Sefer, as a son of Holocaust survivors, themes of survival, keeping our faith and resilience are important ones. The continuity of the Jewish people is paramount. Just as when the Hebrew edition was released, I now am celebrating another milestone - the first of our grandchildren is getting married. The continuity of family is a great consolation, nechama, and a great simcha for us. I dedicate this Sefer to my beloved family - my wife, my children, my grandchildren, and to all future generations.

This is my hope and my simcha. There is a future, Baruch Hashem. Klal Yisrael *will* get past its trials and tribulations collectively and personally, every family, will keep going - and through the words of the Torah, receive encouragement, faith, and resilience.

הודו לה' כי טוב כי לעולם חסדו

We should all merit to see the rebuilding of Jerusalem in all its glory and welcome Mashiach speedily in our days. Amen!

Shlomo Yosef Geliebter
9 Elul 5784

Yom Kippur

I

- ***An explanation of Rabbi Chanina ben Teradyon's martyrdom in sanctification of Hashem's Name***
- ***Why Rabbi Chanina didn't agree to hasten his own death***
- ***Why he agreed to allow the gentile executioner to hasten his death***
- ***His fear that his torments would lead him to question Hashem***
- ***Faith for the generations***

II

Yom Kippur That Falls on Shabbos

- *Yom Kippur in like Shabbos relative to other Yomim Tovim*
- *When Yom Kippur Falls on Shabbos, it is a "Double Shabbos" with Unique Characteristics*
- *What Shabbos and Yom Kippur Have in Common*
- *The Connection Klal Yisroel has with Shabbos and its Power*
- *Yom Kippur that Falls on Shabbos elevates all the Shabbosos of the Year*
- *From Elul to Yom Kippur – The Ascent to the "Mountain of Hashem"*
- *Shabbos elevates us in the "Mountain of Hashem"*
- *The Contrasts Between Yom Kippur and Shabbos complement each other*
- *Spiritual Elevation is the way to attain Atonement and Forgiveness*

- ***An allusion in Parshas Vayakheil***
- ***Yom Kippur that Falls on Shabbos facilitates Teshuva out of Love and Joy***
- ***Seize the Opportunity***

Explaining the martyrdom and death of Rabbi Chanina ben Teradyon

One of the most moving parts of the services of Yom Kippur and Tisha B'Av is the account of the cruel executions of the famous ten martyrs (on Yom Kippur in the *piyyut,* "Eileh Ezkerah" and on Tisha B'Av in the *kinah,* "Arzei Halevanon"). One of these martyrs was Rabbi Chanina ben Teradyon, whose "crime" was to teach Torah publicly. The Romans paid him back in kind by publicly burning him with the Torah scroll that he taught from.

The source of the story is in *Avodah Zarah* 18a:

> *[The Romans] found Rabbi Chanina ben Teradyon, who was sitting and learning Torah and gathering public groups, with a Torah scroll in his lap.*
>
> *They brought him [to be sentenced] and wrapped him in the Torah scroll and surrounded him with bundles of branches and set fire to them. They brought tufts of wool and soaked them in water and placed them on his heart so that his soul would not leave him quickly.*
>
> *His daughter told him, "Father, must I see you like this?" He told her, "If I alone were being burned, the matter would have been difficult for me. But now that I am being burned together with a Torah scroll, He Who seeks [retribution for] the*

insult to the Torah scroll will seek [retribution] for the insult to me."

His students said to him, "Our Rabbi, what do you see?" He told them, "The parchment is burning, and the letters are flying." [They said to him,] "Open your mouth, and let the fire enter [you]." He told them, "Better that He Who gave it should take it and I not harm myself."

The executioner said to him, "My Rabbi, if I increase the flame and take the tufts of wool off your heart, will you promise me life in the world-to-come?" He told him, "Yes." [The executioner said to him,] "Swear to me!" He swore to him. Immediately, [the executioner] increased the flame and removed the tufts of wool on [Rabbi Chanina ben Teradyon's] heart. His soul left quickly. [The executioner] leaped into the fire. A heavenly voice proclaimed, "Rabbi Chanina ben Teradyon and the executioner are destined for the life of the world-to-come."

Rebbe [Rabbi Yehudah Hanasi] wept and said, "There is a person who acquires his world-[to-come] in [only] one hour and someone who acquires his world-[to-come only] after a number of years."

Why Rabbi Chanina didn't agree to hasten his own death but agreed to have a gentile do so?

Rabbi Chanina ben Teradyon was prepared to suffer to sanctify Hashem's name, and to that end he refused to hasten his own death. Nevertheless, he agreed to allow a gentile to do so and, furthermore, promised that gentile the life of the world-to-come. *But why did he agree?*

One may say that when Rabbi Chanina ben Teradyon said that he saw the parchment burning and the letters flying, he was referring not only to the Torah scroll but to himself as well: as his body was being burned, his soul, which is compared to the letters of the Torah, flew up to its Father in heaven, and he wanted his soul to rise with holiness and purity, like letters of the Torah, to eternal life.

However, Rabbi Chanina feared that as a result of the severe torments he was suffering, he would soon question the justice of Hashem and regret having taught the people Torah. He would lose his merits and damage his soul. He feared his soul would no longer be comparable to the lights and letters of the Torah, and he would lose his share in the world-to-come. Thus, he found himself caught in a dilemma. To actively take his life was forbidden, but to continue suffering without a degradation of his spirituality, was no longer possible.

The executioner resolved a dilemma similar to the ram at "Akeidat Yitzchak"

One may say that Hashem opened the eyes and heart of the executioner to see Rabbi Chanina ben Teradyon's holiness and greatness (see *Tosafos* ibid. s.v. *Mah Atah Roeh* on the executioner's exalted spiritual attainment) and in contrast the vanities of this world, and he yearned for truth and the life of the world-to-come. That insight is similar to Avraham gaining sight of the ram caught in the thicket, which made it possible for Avraham to consummate the *Akeidah,* thus sanctifying Hashem's Name completely and with all the necessary pure intentions. To that end, in order that he be spared casting any doubt on Hashem's justice or regretting his earlier good deeds, he was prepared to hasten his death via the agency of another person, and even at the cost of promising a gentile the world-to-come.

Proof from Chananiah, Mishael, and Azariah

When I related this idea to my teacher and dear friend, the *gaon* Rabbi Yochanan Bechhofer, author of *Even Shesiyah,* he agreed that this is certainly the straightforward meaning of this story. He added that this idea is consistent with the Sages' statement about Chanania, Mishael and Azariah, who willingly entered a fiery furnace in sanctification of Hashem's name: "Had Chanania, Mishael, and Azariah been given lashes, they would have worshipped the graven image" (*Kesubos* 33b). In other words, severe torment is a greater test of faith than a martyr's death that only lasts an instant. Rabbi Chanina ben Teradyon wanted to be spared that fate.

Faith for the generations

Rabbi Chanina ben Teradyon defied the Romans by openly teaching Torah to his students, ignoring their edict prohibiting Torah study. The Romans arrested and then subjected Rabbi Chanina to a public tortured slow death, wishing to show the Jews the consequences for disobedience. In the end, the Romans did not break Rabbi Chanina's spirit. Instead, it was Rabbi Chanina in his martyrdom who prevailed. This Jewish hero, through his sacrifice and act of Kiddush Hashem, profoundly affected and inspired those around him and countless others in future generations. Remarkably, this Tzadik's great spiritual presence even sparked a transformation in his Roman executioner who unexpectedly turned from and repented his wicked acts and suddenly desired to enter the world-to-come.

The placement of the tefilla of the ten martyrs at the end of reenactment of the priestly *avodah* service is most fitting because the *avodah* service is considered one of the holiest parts of the Yom Kippur service. The most moving martyrs *tefilla* is a parallel to the binding of Isaac- *Akeidas Yitzchak* by our founding forefather Avraham, a theme which is also prominently featured in the Yom Kippur liturgy.

We will soon encounter the forefather who is most famous for forging the path of faith and *emunah* for the Jewish people. In this Sefer Bereishis, Avraham's unwavering faith and emunah in Hashem and the ten tests of faith he achieved establish the foundation of faith and resilience for his children, the Jewish people.

Rabbi Chanina's story and that of the other ten martyrs remain a testament to the unbreakable spirit and faith of the Jewish people. We are a nation of steadfast faith in Hashem which sustains us through trials and tribulations, persecutions, and attacks throughout the generations. This unbreakable faith is the bedrock of our resilience.

II

Yom Kippur That Falls on Shabbos

Yom Kippur in like Shabbos relative to other Yomim Tovim

The Torah refers to Yom Kippur as שבת שבתון (*Shabbos Shabboson*) (*Vayikra* 16:31, 23:32). There is a well-known interpretation by the *Maharsha* in *Chiddushei Aggados* at the beginning of *Maseches Yoma* where he explains that Yom Kippur is different from all other Yomim Tovim, which are six days in total (Rosh Hashanah - one day, Sukkos - two days, Pesach - two days, and Shavuos - one day). The other Yomim Tovim somewhat resemble the six days of creation because אוכל נפש - work for food preparation is allowed. Yom Kippur, however, is stricter since no work whatsoever is permitted. **Yom Kippur is the Shabbos of the festivals.** All Yomim Tovim are called שבתון (*Shabboson*) in the

Torah, but Yom Kippur is *שבת שבתון (Shabbos Shabboson),* meaning the Shabbos of the Yomim Tovim. This is the secret hinted at by *Maseches Yoma* starting with "Seven days before Yom Kippur..." indicating that Yom Kippur is like the seventh day, akin to Shabbos, as explained by the *Maharsha* there.

When Yom Kippur Falls on Shabbos, it is a "Double Shabbos" with Unique Characteristics

When Yom Kippur coincides with Shabbos, we experience a special "Shabbos Shabboson." We experience the sanctity of both together, and their combination leads to a unique and uplifting experience.

Shabbos and Yom Kippur are different and even contradictory. On Shabbos, there is the commandment "and you shall call the Shabbos **a delight**" - the obligation of - עונג שבת "Shabbos delight," along with an obligation to rejoice and a prohibition against being sad. Conversely, on Yom Kippur, there is a positive commandment to "afflict yourselves" and a negative commandment that "anyone that does not afflict himself shall be cut off..." The experience focuses on self-affliction, restrictions on bodily needs, especially fasting, which is the exact opposite of delight and joy.

On Yom Kippur that falls on Shabbos, there are changes in the prayers due to the sanctity of Shabbos. We do not say "*Avinu Malkeinu*" because requests might cause sadness and interfere with the joy of Shabbos, just as we do not say "*Tachanun*" or even request personal needs, "personal needs we do not ask on Shabbos." There are opinions that we do not say "*Avinu Malkeinu*" on Yom Kippur that falls on Shabbos, so we notice the change from the regular text and remain aware of Shabbos throughout the day (see Aruch HaShulchan).

What Shabbos and Yom Kippur Have in Common

The power of Shabbos is great in restoring levels of holiness and purity and erasing sin, much like Teshuvah and Yom Kippur. Starting with *Kabolas Shabbos,* the Jewish people begin to receive נשמה יתירה - an additional soul. What is included in this additinal soul? With the sin of the Golden Calf, the Jewish people lost two spiritual crowns received at the giving of the Torah. Chazal teach us that Moses guards these two crowns for us as collateral during the week, and on Shabbos, he returns them to us. On Shabbos, we have a temporary respite from the stain of the Golden Calf. But there's more! The Gemara states, "Rabbi Chiya bar Abba said in the name of Rabbi Yochanan, anyone who keeps Shabbos properly, even if they worship idols like the generation of Enosh, they are forgiven" (Shabbos 118b).

The Connection Klal Yisroel has with Shabbos and Its Power

By what merit did we receive "this good gift from the treasure house of Hashem," and how do we draw its power upon us? Shabbos is a covenant between Hashem and the people of Israel. "An eternal covenant... between Me and the children of Israel." On Shabbos, we affirm our belief in the Master of the Universe, the sole creator of the world in six days, who continues its existence. This complete faith is the antithesis of idolatry and nullifies the grave sin of idolatry, and certainly all other sins. Consider this: if we only keep Shabbos on this Yom Kippur, we are guaranteed forgiveness for all our sins just for this alone, beyond the power of Yom Kippur's forgiveness, atonement, and purification! When Yom Kippur falls on Shabbos, there's a double "Shabbos Shabboson," and together they multiply the forces of Teshuvah, forgiveness, atonement, and purification!

Yom Kippur That Falls on Shabbos Rectifies All the Shabbosos of the Year

When Yom Kippur falls on Shabbos, and we all sit in Shul praying, separated and detached from worldly affairs, each of us fulfills the obligation to observe Shabbos perfectly. We keep all the laws of Shabbos in holiness and purity without any distractions, and in doing so, we also rectify all the Shabbosos of the past year that we might not have observed with such strict adherence to all *Hilchos Shabbos*. Thus, on this Shabbos, we can achieve complete Teshuvah through the observance of all Shabbosos of the year, which are all elevated by the Shabbos on which Yom Kippur falls. We have the opportunity on this Yom Kippur that falls on Shabbos to reach new heights in Teshuvah and rectification for the entire year, powered by all the Shabbosos of the year. This is an opportunity we do not want to miss!

From Elul to Yom Kippur – The Ascent to Mount Hashem

Our annual spiritual ascent is akin to the challenge "Who may ascend the mountain of the

Hashem...?" (Tehillim 24:3), to return to the level of Mount Sinai from which we fell. This begins at the start of Elul, when Moshe was commanded to carve the stones that were to become the second Luchos, which happens through "You shall ascend in the morning to Mount Sinai..." (Shemos 34:2). This is a long process of forty days, climbing from one level to the next. We start adding the chapter of Tehillim of "*L'Dovid Hashem Ori*," blowing the shofar, and reciting Selichos. Then we ascend to the level of Rosh Hashanah. On Rosh Hashanah, we pray to be inscribed in the Book of Life. Then, during the עשרת ימי תשובה - Ten Days of Teshuvah, we elevate ourselves to Yom Kippur, which is like "the path to the top of the mountain," where closeness to Hashem brings forgiveness and atonement for all that has passed.

Shabbos Elevates us to the "Mountain of Hashem"

But through the "good gift" of the holy Shabbos, we are like a child living in a high place in the mountains because he was born there. Shabbos elevates us to a higher place on the "mountain of Hashem". By Divine providence, in a year when Yom Kippur falls on Shabbos, there are two days of shofar blowing, which has the virtue of enhancing the awakening to Teshuvah and increasing preparation for Yom Kippur, as explained by the *Rambam* (see Mishneh Torah, Laws of Teshuvah, Chapter 3, Halacha 4, Moreh Nevuchim, Part 3, Chapter 43). In this year when we reach the top of the "mountain of Hashem" through the power of Shabbos, the Divine assistance for this begins already at Rosh Hashanah. When the holy day arrives, we start Yom Kippur with *Kabbolas Shabbos*, already beginning from a higher place. From this higher starting point, our Teshuvah can reach even greater heights.

The Contrasts Between Yom Kippur and Shabbos Complement Each Other

We will quote the pleasant and delightful words of the Bnei Yissaschar in his comments on the Gemara in Shabbos 118b:

"Had [the people of] Israel kept **two Shabosos**, they would have been redeemed immediately (Shabbos 118b), I saw in one holy book that this refers to when **two Shabosos come together**, [it refers to] when Yom Kippur falls on Shabbos. It seems [to me] to explain that it is like 'And they beheld Hashem, and did eat and drink,' which Onkelos translates, 'And they were as happy with their sacrifices which were accepted with favor **as if they ate and drank**.' Yom Kippur is a day without eating or drinking, so there is no 'delight of Shabbos' here, but when the Yom Kippur sacrifices are accepted favorably, there is pleasure like eating and drinking. Thus, there is the observance of both Shabosos, the Shabbos of Yom Kippur with its affliction, and the Shabbos with its eating and drinking. And so in our exile, when our prayers are accepted in place of sacrifices, may Hashem answer and say, 'I have forgiven,' then the combination of both Sabbosos, the affliction, and the pleasure, will lead to immediate redemption, may Hashem hasten it in our days."

To delve deeper into his holy words: The Gemara in Tractate Berachot 31b discusses the relative merits of fasting on Shabbos. "Rabbi Elazar said in the name of Rabbi Yosei ben Zevida that anyone who fasts on Shabbos tears up their [bad] decree for seventy years, yet they must still atone for not fulfilling the commandment of Shabbos delight." If one fasts on Shabbos, they achieve forgiveness and pardon up to the point of canceling a bad decree for seventy years, but then they must atone for not having kept the obligation of Shabbos delight. However, in our case, when Yom Kippur falls on Shabbos, there is nothing to atone for since fasting is obligatory. But the obligation of affliction on Yom Kippur does not merely exempt one from the Shabbos delight; rather, the Bnei Yissaschar teaches us that the joy in our belief that Hashem accepts our prayers on Yom Kippur is the fulfillment of Shabbos delight itself, and in this, there is the full power of Shabbos **combined** with the power of Yom Kippur, enabling one to rise above all sin and deficiency towards complete redemption, may it come speedily in our days.

Yom Kippur That Falls on Shabbos is Teshuvah out of Love and Joy

When Yom Kippur falls on Shabbos, the combination of Yom Kippur and Shabbos allows us to perform Teshuvah on a higher plane. On Yom Kippur that falls on Shabbos, we do not experience the same level of affliction as explained, and therefore, we do not say "*Avinu Malkeinu*" and do not cry out so much. If Yom Kippur leans somewhat towards fear and awe, Shabbos is characterized by love and desire, as stated in the Shabbos prayers even when Yom Kippur falls on it," - באהבה מקרא קודש With **love,** the sacred assembly... והנחילנו ה' אלוקינו באהבה וברצון שבת קדשיך - and endow us, Hashem our L-rd, with **the love and desire** of Your holy

Shabbos." Thus, Shabbos adds love that helps us achieve Teshuvah out of love. Beyond this, there is an inner delight and joy that are an inseparable part of the essence of Shabbos, even when Yom Kippur falls on it, as we have explained. Therefore, it's possible that the Teshuvah on Yom Kippur that falls on Shabbos is of a higher quality, stemming from a place of both love and joy.

For further clarification, let's quote the words of the *Sefas Emes* on Purim of the year 5636 (1876), "On Purim, it is a time for Teshuvah, as it is said that Yom Kippur and Purim are related in terms of rectification... and now, **through joy, we can reach the same level of Teshuvah** that we come to on Yom Kippur through the afflictions." There have always been different paths to Teshuvah. There's the well-known way we do every Yom Kippur, Teshuvah through fasting and various afflictions. But, says the *Sefas Emes,* there is a higher way to do Teshuvah through love and joy, which is present on Purim. According to what we've explained, when Yom Kippur falls on Shabbos, the power of Shabbos adds love and joy, thereby elevating the aspect of Teshuvah on Yom Kippur to be like the Teshuvah of Purim.

Seize the Opportunity

When Yom Kippur falls on Shabbos, there are significant advantages that allow us to reach the highest spiritual peaks. From the onset of Shabbos, we climb from a higher starting point, and by observing Shabbos and focusing on the special qualities of delight and joy that stem from the essence of Shabbos, we elevate our prayers to reach a higher level of Teshuvah, thereby achieving complete forgiveness for our sins. By combining these two forces, which are somewhat contradictory, of Yom Kippur and Shabbos, we can hasten the redemption from our long exile. Amen! May it be Hashem's Will.

Succos and Shemini Atzeres

- ***The reason that the Torah concludes with an allusion to the breaking of the Luchos (the stone tablets containing the Ten Commandments)***
- ***The necessity for the breaking of the Luchos***
- ***Because the Jewish people worshipped an idol, the spiritual crowns that they had received on Mount Sinai were taken away from them***
- ***Moshe broke the Luchos to make the Jewish people cognizant of what they had done***

- ***By striking the rock that gave water, Moshe wished to sanctify the name of heaven before the Jewish people, but he did not succeed***
- ***Reflections Post Simchas Torah 5784***

The final verse of the *Torah* reads, "And for all the great might and all the awesome power that Moshe performed לעיני כל ישראל - before the eyes of all Israel" (*Devarim* 34:12). Rashi comments on the phrase, "לעיני כל ישראל" "before the eyes of all Israel":

> [This alludes to the time that Moshe's] heart stirred him to break the *Luchos* before the eyes [of the Jewish people]. As the verse states, "And I broke them לעיניכם *before your eyes*" (*Devarim* 9:17). And Hashem gave His approval. Thus, [when Hashem told Moshe] "that you broke" (*Shemos* 34), [He meant], "You did well to break them!" (*Shabbos* 87a).

The reason that the *Torah* concludes with an allusion to the breaking of the *Luchos*

On Simchas Torah, which is part of Shemini Atzeres, we complete the final portion of the Torah, which we read publicly in weekly installments over the course of a whole year. This is a day of great celebration above and beyond the fact that it is one of the biblical festivals. The celebration of Simchas Torah is particularly significant because it honors the achievement of continuous and communal Torah study. On its face, Rashi's comment is a very sad way of interpreting the final verse of the *Torah*.

Why did Rashi choose to apply these words of the Sages to conclude the Torah?

The Gemara states (*Shabbos* 87a) that Moshe decided to break the *Luchos* after the *chet ha'egel* (the sin of the golden calf) based on a *kal vechomer* argument, which belongs to the realm of the oral Torah. He reasoned as follows: if the Torah forbids an apostate to eat the *Korban Pesach,* which is only one of the 613 mitzvos, how much more so were the people of Israel, who were at that moment apostates, forbidden from receiving the *Luchos,* which represent the entire Torah (*Shabbos* 87a).

Tosafos states that this is not a flawless *kal vechomer,* because although the *Korbon Pesach* is forbidden to an apostate, in this case Moshe should have given the Jewish people the Torah which would have brought them to repent.

When the Jewish people engaged in *chet ha'egel*, they lost their spiritual crowns, and they were immersed in sin

One may respond to *Tosafos's* argument by saying that the Jewish people had turned their back on the great and awesome event at Mount Sinai where they heard Hashem declare "I am Hashem your G-d." In other words, they were so immersed in the sin of worshipping the *egel* that they could not repent. They were no better than "a person who immerses in a mikveh [to purify himself] while holding a lizard, [which keeps him impure]."

As a result of having served the golden calf, the Jewish people cast off the yoke of accepting the Torah and lost the crowns they received for having accepted the Torah without preconditions through their declaration of "נעשה ונשמע" ("We shall do and we shall hear" [*Shabbos* 88b]). They had plummeted so far that they could not even begin to repent. That is, they were too immersed in evil, **without the Torah to protect them**. The *Ohr Hachaim* tells us (*Parashas Shemos*) that **a person who has reached the fiftieth gate of impurity cannot repent without the power of the Torah.** Similarly, the *Chasam Sofer* writes (at the end of *Yoma*) that **a person who has reached the fiftieth gate of impurity cannot repent on his own but only with the help of heaven.**

The Jewish people were so deeply immersed in the depth of impurity that they could not repent on their own. However, they were undeserving of the Torah, "the light of which impels a person to improve." How then could they elevate themselves? And how would they be saved from their spiritual plight?

Moshe took action to arouse the Jewish people towards repentance

The source of repentance must come from man. Therefore, Moshe, acting as the conscience and representative of the people of Israel, had to devise his own plan. That plan was to inspire the Jewish people to repent. The catalyst for this plan was the dramatic act of breaking the *Luchos,* which would **shock them into an awakening.** The *Luchos* represent the heart of Israel, as in the verse, "Write them upon the tablet (the *luach*) of your heart" (*Mishlei* 3:3). The essential purpose in the breaking of the *Luchos* was to break the hearts of the Jewish people and bring them to repentance, as in the verse, "Hashem will not despise a broken and oppressed heart" (*Tehillim* 51:19). This is in keeping with the statement of the Kotzker Rebbe, "Nothing is as whole as a broken heart."

When Moshe broke the *Luchos,* the Jewish people turned their eyes toward him and toward Mount Sinai, and they recalled the great event of giving of the Torah, which they had forgotten. By breaking the *Luchos,* Moshe caused the Jewish people to pivot from the *egel,* face Moshe and Mount Sinai, confront the gravity of their sin, and were moved to repent.

Moshe's gamble

In truth, Moshe was concerned that after his death he would have to give an accounting for this act. Moshe had broken the *Luchos,* based completely on his own judgement that he had broken the *Luchos,* which were not his, but belonged to Hashem. The *Luchos* were written with the finger of Hashem, and embodied miracles and wonders (such as the final *mem* and the *samech* standing in their place miraculously). How could Moshe even consider breaking them? Seemingly, breaking them would constitute a desecration of the sacred and the erasure of Divine names, and would be similar to dropping a Torah scroll!?

I suggest that Moshe knew well that the *Luchos* were the work of Hashem and the writing was the writing of Hashem, , and that the *Luchos were miraculous and that their* entire existence was higher than nature. And it was ***because*** he knew that, that he concluded it was not necessarily the case that anything negative would result from his breaking them. Moshe prayed that because his entire intent was for the sake of heaven, to bring the nation of Israel to repent, Hashem would not allow any evil to emerge from this act, but only good.

The entire essence of Moshe's breaking the *Luchos* was only "in the eyes of Israel"

Perhaps the entire episode of the breaking of the *Luchos* existed only "before the eyes of Israel" on a physical dimension, but the *Luchos* remained intact in other dimensions of reality. This would explain why the fragments of the *Luchos* were placed in the *aron kodesh*. These fragments accompanied the people of Israel to war, to help them vanquish the enemy. The heavenly power of the shattered *Luchos* continued to exist.

The unbreakable dimension of the *Luchos* is in line with an awesome and wondrous story told about Rabbi Yisrael, the *Beis Yisrael* of Gur, tried to console a survivor of the Shoah who had lost everything. The *Beis Yisrael*, who had also lost his family in the Shoah, told him, "It is written about the breaking of the *Luchos*, 'I broke them before your eyes' and 'before the eyes of all Israel.' This is in keeping with the Sages' comment quoted by Rashi on the verse, '[Yosef] imprisoned [Shimon] before their eyes...' (*Bereishis* 42:24) that Yosef only imprisoned Shimon before [the brothers'] eyes, but when they left, he freed him and fed him and gave him to drink. Similarly, it is only before the eyes of the Jewish people that the first *Luchos* are broken; in reality, however, the *Luchos* remain whole." The *Beis*

Yisrael concluded: "Similarly, we must believe that everything we lost in the Shoah was only 'before our eyes,' and everything still truly exists."

Referring to the original question as to why Rashi would end his commentary on the Torah, interpreting the last three words of the Torah on a sad note, we can now understand that Rashi's uplifting message. Hashem consoled Moshe and informed him that he would not be punished, but on the contrary, "You did well to break them." He promised Moshe that he would be the leader of the people of Israel not only for the generation __ of the desert, but for every generation - and that power of repentance is the secret of our existence. We continue to atone for the sin of the golden calf throughout the generations, until in the future, in the days of Moshiach, no trace of that terrible sin will remain.

The Mei Merivah waters and their connection to the breaking of the *Luchos*

The Torah tells that about forty years after Moshe's breaking of the *Luchos*...

> Hashem spoke to Moshe, saying:
> "Take the staff and gather the congregation, you and Aharon your brother, and speak to

> the rock לעיניהם *before their eyes* so that it will give forth its water...."
>
> Moshe raised his hand and struck the rock with his staff twice, and much water came forth....
>
> And Hashem said to Moshe and to Aharon: "Because you did not believe in Me to sanctify me לעיני בני ישראל *in the eyes of the Jewish people,* therefore you will not bring this congregation to the land that I have given them."
>
> *Bamidbar* 20:8-12

Hashem instructed Moshe to speak to the rock before the "eyes of the nation." Had Moshe performed the action as instructed it would have sanctified the name of heaven. When instead Moshe struck the rock before klal Yisrael, he deprived them of this opportunity to glorify Hashem and increase their Emunah. Hashem therefore decreed that Moshe would not enter the land of Israel.

This ties in to the last verse in the Torah. The Talmud discusses how the entire Torah could have been written by Moshe, since the final verses tell of his death and onwards. Rabbi Shimon states: "Until the point [that Moshe was about to die], Hashem would dictate, and Moshe would repeat and write.

At that point [where Moshe was about to die], Hashem dictated, and Moshe wrote with tears" (Bava Basra 15a).

There is no doubt that when Moshe wrote the verses that describe his death and burial outside the Land, the reason he shed tears was that he recalled having hit the rock before the eyes of the nation, since that is what caused him to die outside the Land.

Hashem consoled Moshe at the very conclusion of the Torah with the words, "לעיני כל ישראל" "before the eyes of all Israel." This phrase hints at the time that Moshe broke the *Luchos* before the eyes of all Israel, and in so doing saved them forever. That is a fine conclusion for the eternal Torah and an ultimate message for the eternal nation.

How is it that we attained complete atonement so that we were not destroyed? That came about when Moshe broke the *Luchos* before our eyes and thus caused us to look toward Mount Sinai and recall the giving of the Torah. That opened the gates of repentance, saved us from destruction, and placed us on the road to complete atonement.

We completed an analysis of the significance of the last three words of the Torah, and how Moshe ensured the survival of Klal Yisroel and the Torah. With the security of the Torah established, we can now proceed to study the Torah from the beginning again.

Reflections Post Simchas Torah 5784

Six years after the original essay on Sukkos - Simchas Torah was published, the Hamas attacks took place on Simchas Torah 5784/October 7, 2023, in Israel. I feel that a postscript to the essay is necessary.

Rashi concludes his commentary on the breaking of the *Luchos,* an interpretation of the final three words of the Torah. We initially struggled with the question of why Rashi chose to write his final commentary on a seemingly sad note. The completion of the yearly reading of the weekly Torah portions, a *siyum,* is a joyous day that calls for great celebration, which we celebrate on Simchas Torah. The horrific attacks on Simchas Torah 5784, was a tragedy compounded by the fact that it occurred on this very day of our festival, when we were to celebrate with great simcha.

In our essay on Simchas Torah, we struggled to find a path to gain an understanding of the complexity of Moshe's breaking of the *Luchos* and to draw lessons of its impact on Klal Yisrael for eternity. Some of these lessons may help us start to navigate through this current tragedy.

We concluded that Moshe's dramatic action was his way of breaking our hearts so we would repent for the *chet ha'egel*. In turn he rescued us and the Torah and saved the world from destruction. Thus, at the end of the Torah we recall Moshe's heroic act, his call for teshuva. As a result of Moshe's actions, we can reach the end of the Torah each year and celebrate the *siyum* of the Torah with tremendous joy. Simchas Torah is that time for joy, but it's also a time for reflection, as Rashi directs us to with his final thought-provoking commentary.

To preserve the *mesorah* and the Torah, Moshe had to break the hearts of Klal Yisrael to stir them to *teshuvah*. In our day, when we experience a tragedy like the one that befell us recently, we need to process it, learn from past experience, and go forward and continue our *mesorah*. That is the only way, to go forward. The only way we can continue, is through simcha. Simchas haTorah, will carry us forward. We need to reflect on where we came from and what we need to do to continue our existence. We must accept that we don't have all the answers. But we do know the rules of our existence and assurances guiding our resilience.

Parashas Bereishis

- **A wonderful explanation of the text of the Friday night Kiddush**
- **Israel without Shabbos is like a man without a wife**
- **Shabbos is the source of faith**
- **The testimonies of the people of Israel, Shabbos, and the Holy One, blessed be He**

An explanation of the text of the Friday night Kiddush

I have thought about why the Jewish people have the ancient tradition of starting Friday night Kiddush with the words "יום הששי" ("the sixth day") before beginning the description of the Sabbath "ויכולו השמים והארץ וגו' " "And the heavens and the earth were completed..." (besides all of the reasons given in accordance with the Kabbalah).

I considered that a straightforward explanation is that the sixth day was the day of the creation of man, and our Sages state, as is well-known, that "You (the Jewish people) are called 'man,' but idolaters are not called 'man'" (*Yevamos* 61a). "Man"—a being who bears the "image of G-d"—applies specifically to Israel, "the nation close to Him." And because of Hashem's great love for the people of Israel, "Hashem said to Moshe: 'I have a good gift in My treasure house. Its name is Shabbos, and I wish to give it to [the people of] Israel..." (*Shabbos* 10b).

Without Shabbos, the people of Israel are incomplete

It is known that the people of Israel are incomplete without Shabbos. Thus, a person who publicly desecrates Shabbos has the status of a gentile (Rambam, *Hilchos Shabbos* 30:15). On the other side of the coin, "Whoever keeps Shabbos in accordance with the halacha, even if he engaged in idol worship like the generation of Enosh, [he] is forgiven.... And if the Jewish people would keep two Shabbosos in accordance with their *halachos*, they would be immediately redeemed" *(Shabbos* 118b).

Shabbos too is incomplete without Israel:

> Rabbi Shimon ben Yochai taught:
>
> > Shabbos said to the Master of the world: "Master of the world, everyone has a spouse, but I have no spouse."
> >
> > Said Hashem to her: "The congregation of Israel is your spouse."
> >
> > When [the people of] Israel stood before Mount Sinai, Hashem told them, "Recall what I said to Shabbos: 'The congregation of Israel is your spouse.'" [This is alluded to by the fact that] the commandment states, "*Recall* the day of Shabbos, to sanctify it" (*Shemos* 20; *Bereishis Rabbah* 11:8).

At the exalted occasion of the giving of the Torah, the sixth day of Creation and Shabbos were united. That is because the sixth day of Creation is associated with the sixth day of Sivan, the day of the giving of the Torah, which occurred on Shabbos:

Reish Lakish said:

> What is the meaning of the verse, "And it was evening and it was morning, 'יום הששי' ***'the*** sixth day'"? [Why does the word "the" appear here [and not in the descriptions of the other days]? It teaches us that Hashem made a stipulation with Creation: "If [the people of] Israel will accept the Torah (on the sixth day of the month of Sivan), then you will continue to exist. But if not, I will revert you back to void and emptiness" (*Shabbos* 88).

The Sages unanimously agree that the giving of the Torah occurred on a Shabbos (*Shabbos* 86b).

The phrase, "*the* sixth day," links the sixth day of Creation with the giving of the Torah, which occurred on a Shabbos. Since the sixth day is so closely associated with Shabbos, at the Friday night kiddush we say the words "the sixth day" before reciting the description of Shabbos.

One may add a deeper understanding of this matter:

Shabbos imbues us with faith

As is known, Shabbos imbues us with the faith that Hashem is one, and that He alone is the Creator and Guide of the universe. Without keeping Shabbos, the people of Israel could not completely attain that faith. The faith of Israel that "Hashem is one and His name is one" was made whole and actual when Hashem descended to Mount Sinai on the Shabbos day on the sixth of Sivan, and "we heard [the first two of the Ten Commandments], 'I am...' and 'You shall have no other...,' from the mouth of the A-lmighty" (*Makkos* 24a). All of that was in the merit of their having already accepted Shabbos at Marah. Because of the merit of keeping Shabbos, they attained the revelation of Divinity that maintains their faith in Hashem—the faith that that He is one and His name is one—on the day of the Shabbos, of the giving of the Torah, which was on the sixth day of Sivan.

As a midrash states (cited by *Tosafos* in *Chagigah* 3b s.v. *Umi K'amkha Yisrael*):

Three bear witness about each other: Israel, Shabbos, and Hashem.

Israel and the Holy One, blessed be He, testify that Shabbos is a day of rest.

Israel and Shabbos [testify] that the Holy One, blessed be He, is one.

The Holy One, blessed be He, and Shabbos [testify] that [the people of] Israel are one and unique among the nations." *Tosafos* continues: "This is what we rely on to say in the *Amidah* of *minchah* on Shabbos "You are one…," even though that paragraph does not make mention of Shabbos (unlike the *Amidah* of *maariv* and *shacharis* on Shabbos)".

Parashas Noach

- **The reason for the 26 repetitions of "כי לעולם חסדו - for His (Hashem's) kindness is forever" in Hallel Hagadol (Tehillim 136)**
- **The difference between Noach and Avraham is that Noach required Hashem's support, whereas Avraham did not**
- **An explanation of the disagreement as to whether to judge Noach favorably or unfavorably**
- **The view that judges Noach unfavorably teaches us that a person can be righteous in any situation**
- **Noach did Teshuva out of fear, whereas Avraham did Teshuva out of love**
- **The building of the Ark reflects the years of man's life**

Shabbos *Parashas Noach* was the last Shabbos of my father's soul upon this earth. Being a Gerrer chasid with every fiber of his being, he gave a talk every Shabbos in the Gerrer *shtiebel* on the Torah insights of the *Sefas Emes*. In order to elevate my father's soul with the crown of Torah and in order that his "lips should murmur in the grave" (*Yevamos* 97a), I wish to address the particular teaching of the *Sefas Emes* that my father spoke about on his final Shabbos in this world.

My father's words came from the depths of his heart. He spoke about how that week's *parashah* was so hard to process as it was an abrupt change and upheaval going from the creation of the world (in *Parashas Bereishis)* to its near destruction the following week. As a survivor of the Shoah, this especially resonated with him, as he lived through and saw a world built and destroyed. This feeling of despair was compounded by the fact that this speech was taking place during the Yom Kippur war, and he was mourning the loss of so many lives and reliving his own painful memories.

His words still echo in my ears and are engraved on my heart.

The *Sefas Emes* (5651) teaches:

> [Rashi states], "Noach required [Hashem's] assistance to support him."

Our Sages say that the 26 generations preceding the [Jews'] acceptance of the Torah were able to exist only due to the kindness of Hashem. Therefore, Hallel Hagadol contains 26 iterations of "because His *kindness* is forever."

Avraham kept the entire Torah before it was given. Thus, it is said about him, "Who preceded Me, that I will pay?" (*Job* 4:2). [This refers to Avraham, who was unique in that he preceded Hashem's giving of the Torah by keeping the Torah (before it was given). Hashem rewarded him for this (*Bamidbar Rabbah* 14:2)]. Avraham drew forth the Torah's illumination even before the Torah was given. Regarding this, [Avraham] stated, "I have walked before Him" (*Bereishis* 24:40). [Avraham gained this ability through] the power of his self-sacrifice, [which he demonstrated] when he cast himself into the fiery furnace [in sanctification of Hashem's name].

The Torah existed before the world was created, and, [in fact], the world was created with the Torah. But the light of the Torah could not be revealed until after the Exodus of Egypt, when Hashem altered the regular course of nature.

However, since Avraham Avinu [too] went against his nature—i.e., against human nature—[in sacrificing himself for Hashem, he gained the merit of sensing the light of the Torah before it was given. And the Torah shone before him and after him.

Indeed, all of the wonders of the Creator shine from the earliest to the last [generations], and in accordance with one's merit, one can feel the light from the earliest generations to the last (*Sefas Emes*: *Noach* 5651).

What if Noach had been in the generation of Avraham?

The verse states, "Noach was a righteous man, perfect in his generations; Noach walked with Hashem" (*Bereishis* 6:9).

Rashi comments on this:

In his generations. Some of our Sages interpret this favorably: how much more righteous would he [Noach] have been had he lived in a generation of righteous people. And some interpret it unfavorably: in the context of his generation, he was righteous, but had he been in Avraham's generation, he would not have been of any account.

Noach walked with Hashem. But regarding Avraham, the verse states, "I have walked before Him" (*Bereishis* 24). Noach required [Hashem's] assistance to uphold him, but Avraham strengthened himself and walked in his righteousness on his own.

The reason for the unfavorable judgment of Noach

From Rashi's second comment, we see that it is universally acknowledged that Avraham was greater than Noach, and the only question that arises is how Noach would have been viewed had he lived in Avraham's generation. But the question would appear to be of no practical relevance. As such, whereas the view that judges Noach favorably accords with the Torah's tendency to judge people favorably, what impels the view that judges Noach unfavorably? Is this the way of the Torah? What benefit can come from it?

Every person and his good deeds are important to Hashem

It appears to me that this teaches us a great and encouraging lesson: although the level that

Noach reached would have been regarded as absolutely nothing had he lived in Avraham's generation, nevertheless, since he maintained his level in a generation of very wicked people, Hashem viewed him as truly righteous! This provides great encouragement for us who are living in the time of "the footsteps of Moshiach" and are on such a low level compared to the generations that preceded us. Yet because we maintain our level, albeit a lowly one, despite living in a very corrupt world, we are righteous in the eyes of Hashem, and He will certainly hasten to redeem us.

The building of the ark reflects the years of man's life

Rashi comments on the phrase, "Make yourself an ark" (*Bereishis* 6:14):

> [Hashem] has many ways of bringing about relief and rescue. So why did He trouble [Noach] with the construction of the ark? It was so that over the course of the 120 years of its construction, the people of the generation of the Flood would see him working on it and would ask him, "What is the purpose of what you are doing?", and he would tell them,

"Hashem is going to bring a flood upon the world." Perhaps they would repent.

Why did Noach work on the ark specifically for 120 years? This apparently alludes to the human lifespan, for when Hashem decreed that there would be a flood, he also stated that "...[man's] days will be 120 years" (ibid. 6:3). There is a message of hope here from Hashem: He waits until the very end of a person's life for him to repent. "Even if [a person] has transgressed all his days, if he repented on the day of his death and died in repentance, all of his sins are forgiven" (Rambam, *Hilchos Teshuvah* 2:1). As we say in the prayers of Rosh Hashana and Yom Kippur, "Until the day of [a person's] death, You wait for him, [and] if he repents, You immediately accept him."

Noach did teshuva out of fear, whereas Avraham did teshuva out of love

During the Aseres Yemei Teshuvah, we ask Hashem, "Bring us back to You, Hashem, and we will return; renew our days." The *Sefas Emes* writes that "Bring us back to You, Hashem" alludes to teshuvah out of fear, which requires Hashem's assistance, whereas "Renew our days as in the beginning" alludes to teshuvah out of love.

I suggest that this marks the difference between Noach and Avraham. Noach required Hashem's assistance to support him; he entered the ark only after the waters of the flood began falling and forced him to do so. This is because teshuvah out of fear requires assistance. But Avraham, who did not require assistance, was on the level of teshuvah out of love. Out of love, he came to know and love his Creator with complete faith. With that, he succeeded in restoring the holiness that had been lost in the generation of the Dispersal—i.e., the people who distanced themselves [from Hashem] "and traveled from "קדם" "the east" (alternate meaning of *kedem*)." Through teshuvah out of love, Avraham Avinu merited and gave merit to the world so that it became possible to "renew our days כקדם [*k'kedem*] as in the beginning."

The month in which the *parashah* of *Noach* is read is called Mar Cheshvan, for which many reasons have been given. *Mar* means "bitter." One may say that this indicates that we can sweeten the bitterness of our misdeeds by means of our teshuvah during the Days of Rosh Hashana and Yom Kippur. As a result of that, we rise to attain teshuvah out of love, and on Simchas Torah, we gain the influence of the Torah. And with that, we sweeten the bitterness of the month of Cheshvan.

Parashas Lech Lecha

- **The first blessing of the *Shemoneh Esrei* mentions both Avraham and the blessing he received**
- **The reason intent is required in the first blessing of the *Shemoneh Esrei***
- **The widespread custom that when one person blesses another, the other responds with an even greater blessing**
- **A person's intent when reciting a blessing is like an additional blessing to the blessing itself**
- **The word "*bareich*" ("blessing") is the secret of proliferation/ manifolding/ propagation/ amplification/ increase/ multiplication**
- **A person's intent enhances the text of the *Shemoneh Esrei***

- **The first blessing of the *Shemoneh Esrei* is the foundation of faith; therefore, it requires especial intent**
- **A person should recite the words of prayer as though they are coins he is counting (*Semak* 11), such that "whoever changes the coinage that the Sages minted has not fulfilled his obligation" (*Berachos* 40b)**
- **Magen Avraham and Lech Lecha**

The first blessing of the *Shemoneh Esrei* mentions Avraham and the blessing he received

The Torah states:

אַחַר הַדְּבָרִים הָאֵלֶּה הָיָה דְבַר ה' אֶל אַבְרָם בַּמַּחֲזֶה לֵאמֹר אַל תִּירָא אַבְרָם אָנֹכִי מָגֵן לָךְ שְׂכָרְךָ הַרְבֵּה מְאֹד.

1. After these things, the word of Hashem came to Avram in a vision, saying: "Do not fear, Avram. I am your מגן [*Magen*] shield. Your reward is very great."

Bereishis 15:1

When *Anshei Knesses Hagedolah* (the Men of the Great Assembly) instituted the text of the *Shemoneh Esrei,* they concluded the first blessing closes with [מגן אברהם *Magen Avraham*], "Shield of Avraham," a phrase based on the words of this verse. As our Sages said on the verse, "and you shall be a blessing" (*Bereishis* 12:2), "[When Jews pray the *Shemoneh Esrei*], they will invoke your name in concluding the blessing" (*Pesachim* 107b). Thus, we conclude that blessing with the phrase, *Magen Avraha*m - i.e., not only Avraham's name but also the blessing Avraham received, namely, "I am your shield." Perhaps this is why the Sages base their statement on the verse, "Be a blessing": that it was blessing—because not only Avraham's name will be mentioned in the conclusion of the blessing but also the blessing that Avraham received will be mentioned in the conclusion of the blessing. Thus, "and be a blessing."

Our Sages taught (*Berachos* 34b)—and this is codified as the halacha in the *Shulchan Aruch (Hilchos Tefillah* 101:1)—that when a person prays, he must have intent in all of the blessings, but if that proves impossible, then he should at least have intent in the first blessing. If he did not have intent in the first blessing, then, even if he had intent in all of the others, he should repeat the *Shemoneh Esrei*. The Rema cites the *Tur,* who disagrees and writes that nowadays we do not repeat the *Shemoneh Esrei*, because if a person repeats it, he will likely not have intent, and that would constitute reciting a blessing in vain.

The reason that intent is required in the blessing of *Magen Avraham*

We see that the blessing of *Magen Avraham* differs from all the other blessings of the *Shemoneh Esrei* in that it is the only blessing in which lack of intent disqualifies the entire *Shemoneh Esrei* (see responsa of Avraham ben HaRambam 79, who discusses this at length). What is so special about *Magen Avraham*?

Let us begin by discussing the topic of intent overall. The widespread custom is that when a person greets another person and blesses him, the other person responds by adding to the first person's greeting and blessing. For instance, when one wishes "Shabbat shalom" to his fellow, the other party answers, "Shabbat shalom umevorach." And even if he does not add a blessing, he replies with a pleasant expression (in keeping with Shammai's words, *Avos* 1:15).

Understanding the custom that when one person blesses another, the other person responds with a greater blessing.

The straightforward explanation is that if one person responds to a greeting with the same words, he is simply repeating words like a parrot, but with no expression of love or affection. The person who initiated the greeting or blessing expressed love and affection. For the person responding to show love, he must respond with an added language so that he is not merely an echo of the first blessing. He must add a blessing or respond with a pleasant facial expression (and it is stated in the name of the Vilna Gaon that this idea applies not only to blessings, but that whenever a person returns a favor he must do more than he received in order to recompense the other person having been the first to bestow benefit).

The same applies to prayer. When the *shliach tzibbur* proclaims, "Bless Hashem Who is blessed," the congregation does not only respond with the same words but with an expanded formula: "Blessed is Hashem Who is blessed forever." The congregation demonstrates that they are not simply repeating the *shliach tzibbur's* words but paying attention and responding with feeling and love.

The deep idea of a blessing is multiplication and enhancement

The depth of meaning of a blessing is multiplication and enhancement. This is alluded to in the letters of ברך [*bareich*]—"blessing"—as I learned from my teacher, the *gaon* of Israel and its glory, Rabbi Dovid Cohen שליט"א, in the name of the Maharal and R. Chaim of Volozhin.

The word *bareich* consists of the letters [ב *beis* [ר,] *reish* [ך,] *kof*]. Their numerical value is 2, 200 and 20, respectively.

ב: 2 in the ones column.

ר: 2 in the hundreds column.

ך: 2 in the tens column.

This indicates that the entire idea of a blessing is that it adds to a single unit (the number one) to begin with multiplicity (the number two).

When a person recites the *Shemoneh Esrei*, intent is required, because intent is an enhancement of blessing

All that we have written so far applies to audible prayers, in which a person can express his addition. However, the *Shemoneh Esrei* is recited silently. All that we can add is our intent, our heart, our feeling. Hashem, Who sees the heart, hears our intent exactly as though we had added words to the text of the *Shemoneh Esrei*. Our heart makes that addition when it is filled with feeling and love.

Therefore, the Sages were especially exacting regarding the need for intent when reciting *Magen Avraham*, since it is the foundation for everything else. Not only is the blessing of *Magen Avraham* the first blessing—and so it begins with *baruch* and ends with *baruch*, and we bow at its beginning and at its end—it also includes the foundations of faith in Hashem and marks the source of the lineage of all Israel—the *Avos*—of whom the head is Avraham Avinu. Therefore, the blessing of *Magen Avraham* is like the father of a family. It provides the structure of the *Shemoneh Esrei*. Just as an entire building stands on its foundation, and just as the entire body is drawn after the head, so too a person's intent as he recites the blessing of *Magen Avraham* applies to the entire *Shemoneh Esrei*, and all the other blessings are drawn after it.

The foundation of faith requires especial intent

All of this corresponds to the character of Avraham Avinu, who laid the foundation of the faith of Israel. Therefore, the first blessing of the *Shemoneh Esrei*, which concludes with "Avraham," is the foundation of faith. This explains why the Sages were especially exacting about the need to have intent when reciting this blessing. As the *Sefas Emes* writes, we conclude the blessing with the words *Magen Avraham* because Avraham Avinu is the foundation of faith, and that foundation is shielded. It is a faithful peg that will not be moved. The entire Jewish nation is built upon Avraham and drawn after him." Hashem promised him that the essence of who he is will exist in every Jew, and He will shield [that essence to keep] it from harm" (*Sefas Emes*: *Parashas Lech Lechah* 5635).

While we are on the subject of the importance of intent in prayer, I recall that at a *siyum* many years ago, the gaon, prince of the Torah and pillar of halachah, Rabbi Tuvia Goldstein זצ"ל, Rosh Yeshiva of Emek Halachah, spoke about the requirement to have intent in prayer in general and in the first blessing of the *Shemoneh Esrei* in particular. Although he spoke of this in terms of the halachic aspect, his words, which came from the depths of his heart, were leaping flames that made a powerful impression on me that I will never forget.

When a person has intent, the "coinage" of his prayer is "tradable"

I have decided that I too will speak of the importance of intent, employing a metaphor, so that these words will enter our readers' hearts. Our Sages describe the text of the prayers as "the coinage that the Sages minted" (*Berachos* 40b). The words are compared to a coin that is valuable in itself due to the value of the metal of which it is made. So too the text of the prayer is intrinsically valuable in its vast wisdom, depth of intent, and beautiful rhetoric.

But as valuable as the 'coin' of prayer is, like a coin, it is doubtful whether it will be accepted everywhere and in every situation. After all, prayer is the articulation of inanimate words from a preformatted liturgy - i.e., "coined words." No matter how precious the text of prayer established by the Sages, it is only ink on paper, a body without a soul (see *Chovas Halevavos, Shaar Cheshbon Hanefesh* 3:9). Who can guarantee that the Master of all will accept these words and give us what we ask of Him? However after the words of prayer are articulated by a Jew, borne by the wings of his speaking breath that flows from his נשמת חיים soul of life, with the addition of intent, his words of prayer are filled with vitality and transformed into a coin of holy fire that rises and breaks through firmaments and is tradable and accepted favorably by the Master of all, and He answers His nation Israel. (See also an extensive explanation of the "coin of fire" in *Parashas Terumah*.)

Magen Avraham and Lech Lecha

"*Lech lecha*", G-d tells Avraham to leave his homeland and be a stranger in the land of Canaan. According to all, this was one of the ten tests of faith Avraham had to pass. He is our forefather, the trailblazer who set the path for our faith, the belief in one G-d, the Creator, the *Ribbono Shel Olam*.

It is most fitting that the first blessing of *Shemoneh Esrei, Birchas Avos,* concludes with *Magen Avraham* acknowledging Avraham. Birchas Avos starts with recognizing that our G-d is the G-d of our forefathers, Avraham, Yitzchak and Yaakov.

Avos is a *bracha* in belief in and connecting with Hashem. The founder of our faith, Avraham

Aveinu, remains our leader in tefillah—our *shliach tzibur* for Emunah in Hashem. It is important as we discussed earlier that we have proper intent or *kavanah* during this first and foundational blessing. Avraham passed ten tests of faith. Our daily test in faith, is to just to pay attention to the words of prayer that we recite. We can make the words come alive and convert "the coins that our Sages minted" for a uniform text for our *tefilos,* into "coins of fire" that can soar through the heavens to the highest levels. With the proper *kavanah* our prayers will be answered by "Hashem, our G-d and the G-d of our forefathers."

Chamudei Shai on the Torah and Holidays

Eternal Wisdom

Faith & Resilience: Our Jewish story–past, present and future

Parashas Vayeira

I

- **An encompassing explanation of the blessing against sectarians in the *Shemoneh Esrei* instituted by Shmuel Hakatan**
- **The reason it was specifically Shmuel Hakatan who instituted the blessing**
- **Humility, prophecy, and Divine inspiration are all interconnected**
- **How can it be that after Shmuel instituted the blessing, he forgot it?**
- **The reason the *Amidah* is called *Shemoneh Esrei* ("Eighteen") despite having nineteen blessings**
- **Shmuel Hakatan reinstituted that blessing, this time in reference to future troubles**
- **We recite specifically nineteen blessings, because we ask Hashem to rescue us**

from the *goy*, a word that has the numerical value of nineteen

- **The propitious custom of giving nineteen coins to charity**
- **Giving nineteen coins to charity lifts us above nature**
- **"Nineteen" and "amen" have the numerical value of ten in *mispar katan***

II

- **Why Avraham didn't want to heed Sarah's demand that he send Hagar away**
- **Avraham Avinu's quintessential character trait was kindness**
- **Hagar was expelled through the trait of severity**
- **Why the Hashem had to direct Avraham to send Hagar away**

I

An encompassing explanation of the nineteenth blessing of the *Shemoneh Esrei*, the blessing against sectarians, composed by Shmuel Hakatan

The Torah states:

א. וירא אליו ה' באלוני ממרא והוא יושב פתח האהל כחום היום

1. Hashem appeared to [Avraham] in Eilonei Mamrei as he was sitting at the entrance of the tent in the heat of the day.

Bereishis 18:1

The *Sefas Emes* teaches:

"He was sitting at the entrance...."

We have already discussed this praise given to Avraham Avinu - that notwithstanding his attainment of every level of greatness, he was still "sitting at the entrance."

And similarly, the verse states, "Fortunate is the person who hearkens to Me, to watch by My doors every day..." (*Mishlei*

8:34). Without a doubt, a person who hearkens to Him every day attains many wondrous levels. As the verse states, "Fortunate is the person who hearkens to Me...." Nevertheless, [that person] should be "watch by My doors."

Thus does the verse the verse state that [Avraham] "was sitting at the entrance of the tent in the heat of the day," meaning that after all of the great enthusiasm that he had at that vision, he nevertheless sat at the entrance.

Sefas Emes, Vayeira 5638

The *Midrash Tanchuma* teaches:

Every day, a person recites the eighteen blessings. Why eighteen? Rabbi Shmuel bar Nachman said: It corresponds to the eighteen times the patriarchs are mentioned in the Torah.

And should someone tell you [they are mentioned] nineteen [times], because the verse states, "the G-d of Avraham your father and the G-d of Yitzchak, the earth upon which you are lying...," tell him this [verse] does not count because Yaakov is not counted with them.

The nineteenth blessing is the blessing against the sectarians, which was instituted by Shmuel Hakatan (see *Berachos* 28b). Further on, we will discuss this extensively. But first we will begin with a wonderful teaching written by my father זצ"ל in *Hamaor* (Tishrei 5733), discussing at length the connection between humility, prophecy, and Divine inspiration.

Humility, prophecy, and Divine inspiration are interdependent

The Talmud relates:

> Shimon Hapukuli arranged the [already existing] eighteen blessings [of the *Shemoneh Esrei*] before Rabban Gamliel Hanasi in Yavneh.
>
> Rabban Gamliel addressed the Sages: "Is there anyone who knows how to institute a blessing against the sectarians?"
>
> Shmuel Hakatan ("Shmuel the Small") stood and instituted it.
>
> *Berachos* 28b

The reason it was specifically Shmuel Hakatan who instituted this blessing is that he had diminished himself to the point that he did not feel his own self at all. It is specifically such a person, who does not feel himself, his needs, and his desires who is fit to institute the blessing of sectarians, for he does so solely for the sake of heaven.

This is also reflected in another Talmudic passage:

> Rabban Gamliel said, "Bring me seven [Sages] early [tomorrow] morning to the loft [designated for convening a court to intercalate the year]." When he went up early [the next morning], he found eight [Sages there].
>
> He said, "Whoever came up without permission must descend."
>
> Shmuel Hakatan stood up and said: "I am the one who came up without permission. I did not come up to intercalate the year but because I need to learn practical halachah."
>
> Rabban Gamliel told him, "Sit down, my son, sit! You are capable of intercalating all of the years, but the Sages said that only those specifically invited may intercalate the year."
>
> [In truth,] it was not Shmuel HaKatan [who had gone up to the loft without permission] but another person, but he acted [as he did in order to spare that person] embarrassment.
>
> *Sanhedrin* 11a

It was specifically Shmuel Hakatan, who was so humble, who could institute the blessing against the sectarians

The Talmud states further on:

> Once, when [a few Sages] were sitting in the loft in Yavneh, a voice from heaven was bestowed upon them: "There is someone here who is worthy of having the Divine Presence rest upon him, but his generation is undeserving."
>
> The Sages turned their eyes to Shmuel Hakatan.
>
> And when he died, they said of him, "Alas, that pious person, that humble person, who was a student of Hillel."

Thus, we see that a humble person is worthy of prophecy. Indeed, at the time of his death, Shmuel Hakatan revealed that which had earlier been revealed to him via Divine inspiration regarding all of the sufferings that would come upon the people of Israel.

As the Talmud relates:

> At the time of his death, [Rabbi Shmuel Hakatan] said: "[Rabban] Shimon [ben Gamliel, the *Nasi* of the Great Sanhedrin,] and

> [Rabbi] Yishmael, [the Kohen Gadol will die] by the sword; their colleagues [will die by other] executions; the rest of the nation will be despoiled, and great troubles will come upon the world."

One may infer that Shmuel had learned this information much earlier, as he was worthy of having the Divine Presence rest upon him. If that is correct, it explains the continuation of the above passage from *Berachos*, as follows:

> The year after [Shmuel Hakatan composed the blessing against the sectarians, he was serving as the prayer leader and] forgot [that blessing]. He scrutinized it for two or three hours [in an attempt to remember it], and [the other Sages] did not remove him [from serving as the prayer leader].
>
> Why didn't they remove him? After all, Rav Yehudah said in the name of Rav that [a prayer leader who erred [in reciting] any of the [other] blessings [of the *Shemoneh Esrei*] is not removed—but [if he erred regarding] the blessing against the sectarians, he is removed, because we suspect him of being a sectarian.

[The answer is that] Shmuel Hakatan is different, because he is the one who instituted [that blessing].

How could Shmuel Hakatan have forgotten the blessing against the sectarians that he himself composed? In order to answer this, let us first address the question of why this prayer is called "*Shemoneh Esrei*" even though it has included the blessing against the sectarians—a nineteenth blessing—for the past 2000 years?

The reason that the *Amidah* is known as the "*Shemoneh Esrei,*" the "Eighteen," even though it comprises nineteen blessings

The blessings of the *Amidah* are meant to be eighteen in number, as may be seen from the many reasons presented in the Talmud and midrashim. As for the blessing against the sectarians, it was originally instituted as a temporary measure, since the people of Israel were suffering from the sectarians and other enemies, and there was a need for a prayer to Hashem that He break our enemies and subjugate the wicked. The intention was that once the prayer had been answered, it would no longer be recited, and the *Amidah* would again consist of eighteen blessings. Since the blessing against the sectarians was meant to be temporary, whereas the eighteen blessings are eternal, we call the *Amidah* the *Shemoneh Esrei*.

With that, we clearly understand that from the outset when the blessing against sectarians was composed it was instituted only so that sinners in that generation will be eradicated from the earth. However, the year after instituting the blessing, Shmuel Hakatan foresaw with Divine inspiration all of the persecutions the people of Israel would endure during this long and bitter exile, and, as a result, he reinstituted that blessing. But as there had to be a new intention behind the blessing—one relevant to the coming exile and persecutions--heaven caused him to forget the blessing so that Shmuel Hakatan would recompose it with the new intention.

We ask Hashem to rescue us from the goy, a word whose numerical value is nineteen

In addition, one may state that the purpose of the blessing against sectarians is to rescue us from those gentiles who are enemies of the Jewish people. The reason this blessing is the nineteenth, therefore, is because the numerical value of the word [גוי *goy*] (gentile) is nineteen, meaning that by means of the nineteenth blessing, we are rescued from the *goy*.

This explains well the "*segulah*" "auspicious custom," instituted by the Sabba Kadisha (Holy Grandfather), Rabbi Yissachar Ber, the founding Admor of Radoshitz,[3] of giving nineteen coins to charity, equal to the numerical value of the word *goy*. One may say that just as the nineteenth blessing corresponds to the numerical value of *goy*, so too giving nineteen coins to charity will rescue us from the goy in all matters, whether bodily or monetary, including judgments and imprisonment.

The reason for the counsel of the holy rabbi of Radoshitz to give nineteen coins to charity

The Rebbe of Radoshitz writes that as a person gives these nineteen coins, he should recite the verse, "They are a *goy (nation)* devoid of counsel, and they have no understanding" (*Devarim* 32:28). It is clear from this verse that the nation of Israel too is referred to as a *goy*. As the verse states, "Who is like Your nation, like Israel, one *goy* in the earth" (*Shmuel*

[3] Rabbi Yissachar Ber Baron of Radoshitz, also called the Sabba Kadisha of Radoshitz, was born in 5525 (1764-65) and passed away on 18 Sivan 5603 (1843). He was known as a great miracle worker, and there are stories testifying to his healing of the sick and even revival of the dead. See *Niflaos Hasabba Kadisha*.

2 7:23). Clearly, here it is the intent of the Rebbe of Radoshitz that when a person gives nineteen coins to charity, he should recite verses that refer to a *goy* of the other nations, who are unintelligent fools that deny Hashem's providence.

An additional reason for giving nineteen coins: so that the giver will transcend nature

When I first heard about this practice many years ago, it occurred to me that a possible for it is that the number nineteen is one more than eighteen. We typically give eighteen coins out of habit, which becomes second nature, in order to attain the life of the World-to-Come in the best possible way, as eighteen has the numerical value of חי "*chai,*" "life." But here we add a coin beyond what we are accustomed to giving in keeping with the will of the elder Rebbe of Radoshitz. By doing the tzaddik's will, we rise to the level of the life of the world-to-come, which transcends nature. (And since we have acted in keeping with the will of the elder tzaddik, it stands to reason that he prays on our behalf.)

The advice of the holy Rabbi Yitzchak Shmuel Eliyahu Finkler[4] of Radoshitz, the last Rebbe of the line of Radoshitz in Pietrokov, Poland, rescued my mother from certain death at the last moment from evil gentiles a number of times. I believe that he had the supernatural ability to rise above the gentiles and rescue Jews from their hands. Without a doubt, he inherited this ability from his holy grandfather, who was known as a miracle-worker.

---

[4] "Born on 19 Adar 5652 (1892) and perished in the Shoah on 27 Cheshvan 5705 (1944) due to hunger." He learned from the extraordinary Torah authority, Rabbi Menachem Zemba (killed in the Holocaust), and from the brilliant Rabbi Nosson Shpiegelglass. At the age of twenty, he inherited his father's place as Admor in Pietrokov. He reached out to and encouraged poor youth, and he was known for the length of his prayers and his minimal need for sleep. He became famous for his good advice, and even Christians came to consult with him. He loved the Holy Land and donated to the Rabbi Meir Baal Haness Fund. During the Shoah, he risked his life to rescue Jews, encourage their spirit, and urge them to keep mitzvos even under impossible conditions. In addition to his great deeds, his good counsel rescued many Jews. His counsel to my mother delivered her a number of times from certain death at the last moment. His deeds, goodness, splendor, and might, both in general and during the years of wrath in particular, as well as his role in rescuing my mother, are documented in 'One Jew's Power—One Jew's Glory: The Life of Rav Yitzchak Shmuel Eliyahu Finkler, the Rebbe of Radoschitz, in the Ghetto and Concentration Camps' by Yechiel Granatstein, published by Feldheim in 5751.

Another appearance of the number nineteen

One may say the following in a manner of *derush* (homiletics).

When the people of Israel are united with mutual love, when we are as one individual with one heart, we are "one nation in the land," the land of Israel.

We learn that Hashem promised Avraham that if there are 45 righteous people in the five cities of Sodom and Amora, He would not overturn them, because each city would be represented by nine righteous people, and Hashem would join each group of nine to form a quorum of ten, a *minyan*, which would justify the city's existence. The number nineteen is a combination of the letter *yod*, which in *mispar katan* has the numerical value of one, and nine, totaling the number ten.

"Amen" in *mispar katan* is ten

One may add that this is in line with our prayer, "And gather us together quickly from the four corners of the earth to our land." "And Hashem will be King over all the earth... Hashem is one and His name is one" (*Zechariah* 14:9). The numerical value of the word "amen" is 91, which in reverse order is 19. When we combine the digits 1 and 9, they add up to ten. And the *mispar katan* of "amen" is ten.

The Maharal and other holy books state that the number ten is associated not only with holiness but also with the revelation of the power of oneness. When we gather together as a unified group, the many become one. This is alluded to in the letter *yod* (whose numerical value is 10), which is a small dot that truly cannot be divided. In keeping with that, one may add that with the concept implicit in "nineteen," we rise to be "one nation," and with that we gain ascendency over our enemies, as alluded to in the verse in the Megillah regarding the Jews assembling and vanquishing their enemies: "the Jews gathered together" (*Esther* 9:2).

II

The reason Avraham Avinu required a special commandment to send Hagar away

b) Further on in the *parashah*, the verses state:

י. "ותאמר לאברהם גרש האמה הזאת ואת בנה כי לא
יירש בן האמה הזאת עם בני עם יצחק.

יא. וירע הדבר מאד בעיני אברהם על אודות בנו.

יב. ויאמר אלוקים אל אברהם ...כל אשר תאמר אליך
שרה שמע בקלה כי ביצחק יקרא לך זרע.

10. [Sarah] said to Avraham, "Send away this handmaid and her son, because the son of this handmaid will not inherit with my son, with Yitzchak."
11. The matter was very evil in the eyes of Avraham regarding his son.
12. [But] Hashem said to Avraham, "... Everything that Sarah says to you, listen to her voice, because in Yitzchak will your offspring be called."

Bereishis 21:10-12

Rashi explains:

Listen to her קול [*kol*] voice. To the voice of Divine inspiration in her. Thus, we learn that Avraham was secondary to Sarah in prophecy.

***Kol*, "voice," alludes to levels of prophecy**

The Torah states (in *Parashas Lech Lecha*):

1. Sarai, the wife of Avram, had not borne him [children], and she had an Egyptian handmaid whose name was Hagar.
2. And Sarai said to Avram, "Now Hashem has prevented me from giving birth. Come now to my handmaid, perhaps I will be built from her." And Avraham heeded Sarai's קול - voice.

Bereishis 16:2

Rashi comments:

Sarai's קול - voice. The Divine inspiration in her.

Thus, we see that the word קול "voice" indicates levels of prophecy and Divine inspiration (as we will explain at length in *Parashas Toldos*).

Why Avraham heeded Sarah regarding taking Hagar but not regarding sending her away

The following requires study:

In *Parashas Lech Lecha,* when Sarah told Avraham to take the drastic step of bringing an Egyptian handmaid into the congregation of Israel, he immediately nullified his viewpoint before that of the Divine spirit in her. But in this *parashah,* when Sarah wanted to protect the purity of the congregation of Israel by expelling the handmaid and her son so that Yitzchak would remain righteous and the congregation of Israel would be built of holy seed blessed by Hashem alone, Avraham Avinu was not prepared to nullify his viewpoint before Sarah's Divinely inspired words until Hashem Himself commanded that of him and told him that Sarah is greater than him in prophecy. What was the difference between these two prophecies of Sarah?

As is known, the trait of Avraham is that of kindness. As the verse states, "Give truth to Yaakov, kindness to Avraham..." (*Micah* 7:20). We see this clearly at the beginning of the *parashah,* where Avraham interrupted his communion with Hashem in order to invite guests (see *Shabbos* 127a). Kindness was the essence of his being, and it served as his benchmark for what constitutes "truth and righteousness."

Avraham engaged in acts of kindness on his own initiative, but Hashem had to command him to engage in an act of severity

When Sarah asked Avraham to bring Hagar into their household, she was acting with supreme kindness. She relinquished her status and brought a competitor into her home in order to build the congregation of Israel. Since this was in line with "the world [being] built on kindness" (*Tehillim* 89:3), Avraham certainly saw truth and justice there, in keeping with his trait of kindness.

However, in this *parashah* Sarah asked Avraham to perform a deed on the level of severity, the opposite of the trait of kindness: to expel the handmaid. Avraham's trait of kindness could not accept that as truth and justice until Hashem informed him that Sarah's prophecy reached higher than his trait of kindness, that it reached up to the Divine truth that now demanded the trait of severity to expel Hagar and Yishmael, and thus remove them from the congregation of Israel.

Chamudei Shai on the Torah and Holidays

Eternal Wisdom

Faith & Resilience: Our Jewish story–past, present and future

Parashas Chayei Sarah

I

- **A new explanation as to why Avraham did not confer with Sarah before the *Akeidah*; seemingly justice and common decency would have demanded that he do so.**
- **Since Avraham received an explicit command from G-d about the *Akeidah*, he had no more questions.**

II

- **"And Hashem blessed Avraham with everything": that is the essential point.**
- **The reason that we recite the verse, "And Avraham was old," after Hallel.**
- **The reason that we do so specifically after Hallel on Rosh Chodesh.**
- **The meaning of the verse, "Do not cast us away at the time of old age."**

I

A new explanation of why Avraham did not consult with Sarah before the *Akeidah*; seemingly, justice and common decency would have demanded that he do so

The Torah states:

ב. ויבוא אברהם לספוד לשרה ולבכותה:
(בראשית כג, ב)

2. "And Avraham came to eulogize Sarah and to weep over her" (*Bereishis* 23:2).

Rashi comments:

> **To eulogize Sarah and to weep over her.** Her soul flew out of her, and she died as a result of her receiving the news about the *Akeidah*, that her son had been prepared to be sacrificed and indeed was almost sacrificed.

We see from this Rashi that Sarah was unaware of G-d's instruction to Avraham to offer up Yitzchak as a sacrifice, and that when she heard that Yitzchak had been prepared as a sacrifice, she was overcome with such intense emotion that she passed from this world.

My teacher, Rabbi Dovid Cohen states that a mother's compassion—רחמים (*rachamim)*—derives from her womb רחם (*rechem).* A mother has an especially strong compassion for her child because her womb, which is the source of compassion, bore that child.

Knowing the great compassion a mother has for her child, and knowing that Sarah was (presumably) unaware of G-d's instruction to him concerning the *Akeidah,* why didn't Avraham confer with Sarah before he went to perform the *Akeidah*? Wouldn't justice and common decency have demanded that he do so?

With regard to justice, our Sages say there are three partners in the creation of a person: The Holy One, blessed be He, the person's father, and the person's mother (*Kiddushin* 30b). Since the mother is as much a partner as Hashem and the father, and Avraham knew of the upcoming *Akeidah,* shouldn't Sarah have been informed of it as well? Furthermore, Sarah was greater in prophecy than Avraham, as Rashi states on the verse, "Everything that Sarah says to you, listen to her voice" (*Bereishis* 21:12). Therefore, it would have only been right for Avraham to have conferred with Sarah.

From the perspective of common decency as well, it seems that Avraham should have informed Sarah of the *Akeidah.* We know that Avraham was a man of kindness and love. He should have felt compelled by that kindness and love to discuss this difficult decision with his wife, who, after having been infertile for ninety years, had finally had a child and endured pregnancy and birth in her old age.

When one hears directly from Hashem, there is no room for questions

But since Avraham heard the command to perform the *Akeidah* directly from Hashem, it would have been wrong for him to confer with Sarah, even though she was his partner in the creation of Yitzchak, and even though she was greater than him in prophecy. Similarly, years later, when Yaakov mourned what he believed to be Yosef's death, Yitzchak knew by Divine inspiration that Yosef was alive, but he nevertheless did not inform Yaakov of this, because he saw that G-d had withheld the information from Yaakov.

II

"Hashem had blessed Avraham with everything" so that everything would be blessed by Avraham.

א. ואברהם זקן בא בימים וה' ברך את אברהם בכל:
(בראשית כד, א)

1. "And Avraham was old, advanced in days, and Hashem had blessed Avraham with everything" (*Bereishis* 24:1).

The *Sefas Emes* teaches that in this blessing, "everything" refers to the central point from which everything receives blessing. Thus, after Avraham received this blessing, he and his offspring could be the source of blessing for all Creation. The verse's reference to Avraham's old age indicates that in the course of all his days, Avraham nullified himself to Hashem and, in that way, became a vessel to contain all the blessings in the world.

(In keeping with the Ramban's comment on the phrase describing Yitzchak as having been "old and sated with days" [*Bereishis* 35:29]), one may add that all of Avraham's days were completely filled with good, since the righteous do not desire luxuries but only that which they need to serve Hashem. Avraham was filled with all of the good that he desired, sated with spirituality.

From the words of the *Sefas Emes*, we will understand why this verse is recited on Rosh Chodesh

With this explanation of the *Sefas Emes,* we can explain the custom (see *Mishnas Chasidim,* Maseches Rosh Chodesh 2:6) of reciting this verse after Hallel as a spiritual catalyst ("*segulah*") for attaining long life: We say this verse specifically after Hallel of Rosh Chodesh because Rosh Chodesh is a time of renewal. The root of the word "*chodesh,*" "month," is "*chadash,*" "new," for when the moon is renewed, there is a renewal of life. For this reason, in *Birkas Hachodesh,* our prayer for the upcoming new month, we say, "Give us long life, a life of peace, a life of goodness, a life of blessing...." Because praying for a new month is also the time to pray that our days will be sated, that we will live a long life filled with every manner of goodness from the Source of all blessing.

The custom of reciting the abovementioned verse sheds light on our Sages' statement that a person who meets a friend after a hiatus of thirty days recites the blessing of "Shehechiyanu" (*Berachos* 58b). The reason for specifying a thirty-day time period is because every thirty days — the average length of a month — marks a period of renewal.

"Do not cast us away at a time of old age" is a request that old age not come upon us prematurely

The prayer, "Do not cast us away at a time of old age; when our strength fails, do not forsake us" (Siddur; cf. *Tehillim* 71:9), is simply a request of Hashem that He not abandon us at the end of our days. But it may also be read as a prayer that Hashem not cast us into premature old age.

Parashas Toldos

I

- **A deep explanation why our prayers contain many verses that were spoken by idolaters**
- **Whatever is mentioned in Tanach is holy**
- **"She took the veil and covered herself" (*Bereishis* 22:65) is similar to a *badeken* (the veiling of a bride)**
- **The three first blessings of the *Shemoneh Esrei* correspond to the three Patriarchs (the *Avos*)**
- **It is specifically the prayer of Yitzchak, who represents the trait of strict justice, which can be transformed into the trait of compassion**
- **With faith, we see that everything is kindness**

- **After awakening from sleep, which is a sixtieth part of death, we thank Hashem for having awakened us "with great mercy"**

II

- **A profound reason why Rivkah did not reveal her prophetic knowledge to Yitzchak**
- **Yaakov had to attain Yitzchak's blessings in a deceptive manner**
- **The "voice" mentioned in relation to Rivkah is a term for prophecy**
- **Sources in Onkelos, *Tosafos* and the *Ohr Hachaim* regarding Rivkah's "voice"**
- **The word Rivkah used, *alai*, "upon me," is an acronym for "Esav, Lavan, Yosef"**

I

The Torah states:

כא. ויעתר יצחק לה' לנכח אשתו כי עקרה היא ויעתר לו ה' ותהר רבקה אשתו:
בראשית כ"ה:כ"א

21. Yitzchak prayed to Hashem opposite his wife because she was barren. Hashem heeded him, and Rivkah his wife conceived.
Bereishis 25:21

Chizkuni writes, quoting the midrash:

> Why was Rivkah barren? So that the nations [as represented by her birth family] should not say, "The prayer that we recited on behalf of our sister, 'Our sister, may you become thousands of myriads 'אחתנו את היי לאלפי רבבה' (*Bereishis* 24:60), bore fruit." Rather, "Yitzchak prayed… and Hashem heeded *him*."

In light of this interpretation, it is difficult to understand why we have the custom of blessing the bride at the time of the *badeken* with the blessing of "אחתנו": "Our sister, may you become thousands of myriads." Since the phrase, "and Hashem heeded *him*" teaches that we should not think it was Lavan's blessing to Rivkah that came true, why do we have the custom of blessing a bride with those very words?

Why did our Rabbis insert verses stated by idolaters into the text of the siddur?

It is similarly surprising that every day when we enter shul, we recite the verse, "How goodly are your tents, Yaakov," מה טבו אהליך יעקב משכנתיך ישראל (*Bamidbar* 24:5), which was stated by the evil Bilaam,[5] and that on Simchas Torah we sing the words, "Who is this and where is he?" (*Esther* 7:5), which Achashverosh said referring to Haman, but which we say referring to Hashem, and to which we respond, "This is my G-d and I will glorify Him!"

---

[5] See Responsa Maharshal 64:

> When I come to the Beis Hakneses (synagogue) in the morning, I begin with the verse, "And I, in the greatness of Your kindness..." (*Tehillim* 5:8). I skip the first verse, "How goodly are your tents," (מה טבו...)
>
> (which Bilaam said as a curse, as stated in *Perek Cheilek* (*Sanhedrin* 105b: "Rabbi Yochanan said: From the blessing of that wicked person, you learn what was in his heart. He wished to say that they should not have synagogues and study halls, [and he was forced to say instead,] 'How goodly are your tents, Yaakov.' [He wished to say that] the Divine Presence should not rest upon them, [and he was forced to say instead,] 'And your dwelling places, Yisrael'...").
>
> This will be discussed further on.

The very fact that these verses appear in Tanach constitutes their holiness

One may answer that since these words are written in Tanach, they are holy, and we have permission to make use of them. When these words are spoken with pure intent by the people of Israel, a holy nation, then everything they lacked when they were spoken by the nations of the world, who sullied them, is completed and rectified. They were initially spoken by the nations of the world by Divine design - namely, as "a descent for the sake of an ascent," so that they would eventually be transferred from the realm of unholiness into the realm of holiness and be entirely rectified. When they are spoken by a Jew, they rise and return to their root.

Sefer Taamei Haminhagim states that customarily it is the rabbi or an important member of the community who blesses the bride with the words, "Our sister, may you be...." One may explain that this is because such a person has the ability to transform these words so that the bride will be blessed with "our sister" in keeping with the proper intent. Similarly, by incorporating the verse, "How goodly are your tents," into the siddur, the Sages transformed it to holiness .

"She took the veil and covered herself," similar to a *badeken*

Immediately after Rivkah was blessed by her brother and mother, she traveled to the Holy Land. There, "Yitzchak went out to pray in the field towards evening, and he raised his eyes and he saw and behold, camels were coming" (*Bereishis* 24:63). When he saw that Eliezer had returned with Rivkah, he realized that she was his bride, and he prayed that their marriage should be successful. And when Rivkah saw her groom Yitzchak, "she took the veil and covered herself," which is similar to a *badeken*. That was "a deed of the forefathers that serves as a sign for the children": i.e., that we recite that blessing at a *badeken*. In that generation, it took twenty years before Yitzchak elevated this blessing to its supernal root, when he and Rivkah finally had their children. But ever since Yitzchak introduced the practice of reciting that blessing at weddings, its impact is felt immediately.

One may delve more deeply into this by explaining the verse, "Yitzchak prayed to Hashem opposite his wife," in accordance with our Sages' statement, "Avraham instituted the prayer of *shacharis*..., Yitzchak instituted the prayer of *minchah*..." (*Berachos* 26b).

The three first blessings of the *Shemoneh Esrei* correspond to the three *Avos*

Pirkei Derebbe Eliezer states that the first three blessings of the *Shemoneh Esrei* correspond to the three *Avos* (chapter 31 see also *Seder Hayom, Kavanas Shemoneh Esrei*). The first blessing, "Shield of Avraham," corresponds to Avraham, whom the Holy One, blessed be He, shielded and rescued from Or Kasdim. The second blessing, "He Who revives the dead," corresponds to Yitzchak, whose soul left his body at the time of the *Akeidah* and whom Hashem revived, which made Yitzchak aware that in the future Hashem would revive the dead (hence his recitation of this blessing). And the third blessing, "the holy G-d," corresponds to Yaakov, who is the root of holiness, in that his holiness is tripled, since in addition to his own holiness he possesses the holiness of Avraham and Yitzchak.

As is well-known, Yitzchak represents the trait of strict justice. How is it, then, that the second blessing speaks of Hashem's compassion: "He provides life with kindness, revives the dead with vast compassion..."?

That may be understood in light of the Sages' statement that *vayetar*, the Hebrew verb for "prayed" in the verse "Yitzchak prayed," is related to *eter*, "pitchfork," indicating that "just as a pitchfork turns over the grain from one spot to another, so does the prayer of the righteous turn over the traits of the Holy One, blessed be He, from anger to compassion" (*Yevamos* 64a). Yitzchak's trait of strict justice - מדת הדין - then, is transformed to kindness and compassion - מדת הרחמים. (See *Sefas Emes* [5653], s.v. *Vayetar Yitzchak*.)

It is precisely Yitzchak who by means of prayer transforms strict justice to compassion

One may suggest that it was therefore Yitzchak who instituted the prayer of *minchah*, which is recited toward the evening, the time of strict justice, in order to transform that strict justice into compassion. Similarly, the Sages state that it is Yitzchak who will in the future speak on behalf of the children of Israel and rescue them from the trait of strict justice (*Shabbos* 89b). Only a person of great might (גבורה) can transform strict justice to compassion.[6]

Thus, Yitzchak, through the power of his prayer, had the ability to transform the state of his wife's barrenness to motherhood.

Yitzchak blessed Yaakov with the words, "May Elokim give you" (*Bereishis* 27:28). That name of Hashem corresponds to the trait of strict justice. Yitzchak's intent was to grant Esav—who is also associated with that trait—the power to transform strict justice into compassion. But when Yitzchak realized that he had actually blessed Yaakov, he immediately sanctioned that blessing, saying "Indeed, he shall be blessed" (ibid. 33), because he understood that it was Hashem's will to link the trait of strict justice with the trait of Yaakov, which is compassion. And in that way, strict justice was transformed to compassion in the last of the *Avos*. When this occurred, states the *Zohar* (*Parashas Emor*), all the worlds were filled with rectification

---

[6] The Ari and others teach that although in this world the halachah is in accordance with the view of the School of Hillel, which is associated with kindness, in the future the halachah will be in accordance with the view of the School of Shammai, which is associated with strict justice. However, that is not for the reason discussed here but for another reason: In the messianic future, the world will be purified and rise to the level it was initially supposed to have reached when "it arose in [His] thought to create [the world] with the trait of strict justice" (*Bereishis Rabbah* 1:4). In the messianic future, the world will be able to exist on that exalted level.

and gladness - תיקון וחדוה. Thus does the verse say, "Because from within Yitzchak will your offspring be called" (ibid. 21:12) - meaning, as the Sages explain, from only some of the offspring of Yitzchak —"from within Yitzchak"—but not from all of Yitzchak (*Sanhedrin* 59b). That is, Yitzchak is associated specifically with Yaakov and not with Esav.

The trait of kindness exists even in the presence of death

Sleep is associated with death. That's why every morning we thank the Holy One, blessed be He, "that You returned my soul to me with graciousness; vast is Your faithfulness." Indeed, the Holy One, blessed be He, responds "with graciousness" to this sleep of ours, this sort of death-like state we slip into, which corresponds to strict justice. By returning our soul to us with graciousness, the Holy One's strict justice blends with His compassion. "Vast is Your faithfulness" may be interpreted to mean that we are granted the amelioration of strict justice as a result of our vast faith that the Holy One, blessed be He, will give us life every day anew.

In the second blessing of the *Shemoneh Esrei*, we say, "He Who revives the dead with abundant compassion." Death is strict justice, as seen by the fact that upon hearing the news of someone's death we recite the words, "Blessed is the true Judge." But when it is blended with "vast compassion," the dead are revived. And that is in the merit of our faith that the Holy One, blessed be He, will revive the dead. Therefore, the blessing continues with the words, "and You are faithful to revive the dead."

Every day before going to sleep, our faith — via which we merit Hashem's kindness — is renewed

Our faith is renewed every night when we go to sleep, which is, as the Sages say, a 60th of death (*Berachos* 57b). We have faith in Hashem and thus we deposit our soul with Him, and we recite the words, "In Your hand I deposit my soul; You have redeemed me, Hashem, true G-d," which means that He is faithful to return the deposit to us the next morning, and when He does, we recite the blessing, "He Who returns souls to dead corpses."

All of that is alluded to in the verse, "They are new in the morning; vast is Your faithfulness" (*Eichah* 3:23). That is similar to the phrase, "In His goodness, He constantly renews every day" (siddur). When we are asleep it is as though we are dead, and after the Holy One, blessed be He, returns our souls to us in the morning we are renewed like a new-born child. And all of that is in the merit of our vast faith in Hashem.

II

The Torah states:

ה. וְרִבְקָה שֹׁמַעַת בְּדַבֵּר יִצְחָק אֶל עֵשָׂו בְּנוֹ וַיֵּלֶךְ עֵשָׂו הַשָּׂדֶה לָצוּד צַיִד לְהָבִיא:

ו. וְרִבְקָה אָמְרָה אֶל יַעֲקֹב בְּנָהּ לֵאמֹר הִנֵּה שָׁמַעְתִּי אֶת אָבִיךָ מְדַבֵּר אֶל עֵשָׂו אָחִיךָ לֵאמֹר:

ז. הָבִיאָה לִּי צַיִד וַעֲשֵׂה לִי מַטְעַמִּים וְאֹכֵלָה וַאֲבָרֶכְכָה:

ח. וְעַתָּה בְנִי שְׁמַע בְּקֹלִי לַאֲשֶׁר אֲנִי מְצַוָּה אֹתָךְ:...

יא. וַיֹּאמֶר יַעֲקֹב אֶל רִבְקָה אִמּוֹ הֵן עֵשָׂו אָחִי אִישׁ שָׂעִר וְאָנֹכִי אִישׁ חָלָק:

יב. אוּלַי יְמֻשֵּׁנִי אָבִי וְהָיִיתִי בְעֵינָיו כִּמְתַעְתֵּעַ וְהֵבֵאתִי עָלַי קְלָלָה וְלֹא בְרָכָה:

יג. וַתֹּאמֶר לוֹ אִמּוֹ עָלַי קִלְלָתְךָ בְּנִי אַךְ שְׁמַע בְּקֹלִי וְלֵךְ קַח לִי:

בראשית כ"ז:ה' - י"ג

5. Rivka heard Yitzchak speaking to Esav his son, and Esav went to the field to hunt game to bring [it].
6. And Rivka spoke to Yaakov her son, saying, "Behold, I heard your father speaking to Esav your brother saying:

7. 'Bring me game and make me delicacies, and I will eat, and I will bless you.'

8. "And now my son, listen to my voice, to that which I command you."...

11. And Yaakov said to Rivkah his mother, "Behold, Esav my brother is a hairy man, whereas I am a smooth man.

12. "Perhaps my father will touch me, and in his eyes I will be as a deceiver, and I will bring a curse upon myself and not a blessing."

13. His mother said to him, "Upon me is your curse, my son, but listen to my voice, and go, bring [them to] me."

Bereishis 27:5-13

Why Yaakov Heeded Rivkah's words

This episode is difficult to understand—both from the standpoint of Rivkah acting as she did and from the standpoint of halachah.

To begin with, why didn't Rivkah tell Yitzchak her opinion of Esav and that she opposed Yitzchak blessing him? And how could she assure Yaakov that no evil would befall him, given that Yitzchak would realize that Yaakov had taken the blessings by deception?

And second, how could Yaakov heed Rivkah's voice to act against Yitzchak's will, when the halachah is that when a person's parents disagree about what he should do, he must heed his father, since "both you and your mother are obligated to honor your father" (*Kiddushin* 31a)?

The answer is inherent in the fact that—as stated earlier regarding the verse, "Everything that Sarah says to you, listen to her voice" "שמע בקולה" – the word "voice" often refers to prophecy, Divine inspiration, or a *bas kol* "בת קול" (a voice from heaven).

Rivkah's "voice" was of a prophetic nature

In Rivkah's words to Yaakov, "And now my son, listen to my voice (שמע בקולי) , to that which I command you," the word "voice" is superfluous and thus comes to teach something beyond the simple meaning of the text. It comes to teach us that these instructions of Rivkah were words of prophecy. "To that which I command you" thus indicates not only the commandment to honor/obey one's mother but also the commandment to heed the instructions of a prophet. And the law regarding a prophet is, "You shall heed him" (*Deuteronomy* 18:15). That is, a prophet has the authority to command a temporary abrogation of the Torah. Rivkah's prophetic instruction thus overrode the halachah that "both you and your mother are obligated to honor your father" and also overrode Yaakov's concern about acting deceitfully.

And just as the word "voice" indicates that Rivkah spoke prophetically, so does the phrase "Rivkah heard" indicate prophetic hearing, and so everything that she did, said, and promised throughout this entire *parashah,* was rooted in prophesying.

Support for this idea may be found in the writings of our holy rabbis:

The *Ohr Hachaim*

The *Ohr Hachaim* (*Bereishis* 27) teaches:

5. **And Rivkah heard....** The verse is telling us that Rivkah was a prophetess.... Therefore, [the verse] states, "and Rivkah *hears...,*" [meaning that she was in an ongoing state of prophetic hearing], and not "and Rivkah *heard....*"

6. **And Rivkah spoke....** The word "and" indicates that she was attuned to the Divine inspiration resting upon her (because the "and" is superfluous).

8. **"And now."** "Although there is something deceitful in these words, you must nevertheless listen to my voice—meaning, besides the obligatory mitzvah of honoring one's father and mother, which is a positive commandment, [what I am saying] is prophecy." And [the Torah] writes regarding the words of a true prophet, "you shall heed him" (*Devarim* 18:15). It was in this context that [Rivkah] said, "Listen to my voice - שמע בקלי." And we have already written that a prophet is justified when he [issues a command] to temporarily transgress one of the mitzvahs of the Torah.

Onkelos and *Tosafos*

Following the explanation I presented above, I came upon newly published writings (5783) of the *Baalei Tosafos,* in which Rabbeinu Shlomo ben R. Shmuel of Wurzburg writes as follows:

5. **And Rivkah hears.** Through prophecy....
8. **"And now, my son, listen to my voice."** "To the voice of prophecy in me, because

> it is for your sake that Divine inspiration has rested upon me, so that you may receive the blessings. And I was also told through prophecy that the Holy One, blessed be He, treats a person in accordance with his measure. 'By the measure with which a person measures, so is he measured' (Mishna, *Sotah* 1:7). Esav, your brother, is deceiving your father, telling him: 'Father, how do we separate *terumah* from salt? How do we tithe the straw?' The Holy One, blessed be He, will treat him in the same measure. As such, you are to take the blessings from him by deceit, so that he will not have them."

Similarly, Targum Rabbi Yonason ben Uziel renders the words, "Rivkah heard," as, "[She heard] with Divine inspiration."

Similarly, Targum Onkelos translates *Bereishis* 27:13 as:

> And his mother said to him, "It was told to me through prophecy that the curse will not come upon you, my son. But obey me and go, bring me."
>
> *Bereishis* 27:13

Alai, "upon me," is an acronym for "Esav, Lavan, Yosef"

The Vilna Gaon states that the word *alai*, "upon me," in the verse, "Upon me is your curse, my son," is an acronym for "Esav, Lavan, Yosef," and that Rivkah was communicating to Yaakov that he would suffer in relation to these three men, but no more than that. But where did the Vilna Gaon derive this from? Perhaps it is based on Onkelos's linkage of the word *alai* with prophecy. The Vilna Gaon is merely adding some detail to the nature of that prophecy.

According to this interpretation of *alai*, the question of how Rivkah could have made herself vulnerable to a curse ceases to exist, since in fact she did not do so at all but was speaking words of prophecy.

Why didn't Rivkah inform Yitzchak of her prophetic knowledge?

Rivkah did not tell Yitzchak of her prophetic knowledge that Esav was unworthy of receiving the blessings, because, as stated by R. Shlomo ben R. Shmuel of Wurzburg, she had learned prophetically that that Yaakov was to receive the blessings in a deceitful way, so as to punish Esav for his deceitful behavior.

In addition, one may state that Rivkah wanted Yitzchak to be in a calm and joyful state of mind so that the Divine Presence would rest upon him as he blessed Yaakov. She was concerned that were she to tell Yitzchak that Yaakov was the son who should receive the blessings and that Yitzchak's hopes for Esav had been in vain, Yitzchak would fall into melancholy and consequently be deprived of the Divine inspiration necessary to transmit the blessings and affect the future of the people of Israel. Rivkah's intent was in fact realized, and Yaakov received the blessings at a time when Yitzchak was tranquil and in the highest spiritual state. In order to reach that state, Yitzchak first ate and drank, so that afterwards "my soul will bless you." Proof that Yitzchak was in an elevated state when Yaakov entered his presence is that Yitzchak was aware of the scent of the Gan Eden that entered the room together with Yaakov (Rashi on *Bereishis* 27:27). (Perhaps one may further suggest that Yitzchak's statement, "the voice is the voice of Yaakov" [ibid. 22], indicates that Yitzchak sensed the Divine inspiration resting upon Yaakov.)

Esav, on the other hand, was destined to receive his blessings at a time when his father was unsettled and unsure. Thus, when Esav came to receive Yitzchak's blessings, Yitzchak was confused and afraid. "Yitzchak trembled very greatly" [ibid. 33]," and he did not want to bless Esav at all. And presumably, even when Yitzchak did agree to bless Esav, he remained in an unsettled state of mind.

Parashas Vayeitzei

I

- **An explanation of dreams and prophecy**
- **The twelve stones that became one**
- **With unity, we gain protection**
- **The word *avanim*, "stones," alludes to the unity of all the tribes**
- **Unity comes about by means of faith, and that is unity's greatness**
- **An explanation of the prayer, "Guardian of Israel"**
- **Yaakov entered into darkness to help us in the darkness of the exile**
- **Yaakov wished to reveal the end so that his descendants would be able to withstand the difficulties of the exile**
- **Yaakov was uncertain why the Divine Presence left him**

II

- **Another miracle regarding the stone and the construction of the House of Israel**

III

- **A deep look at Rachel's marriage**
- **Lavan feared Yaakov's spiritual and physical power**
- **Lavan was a miser who insisted on receiving what he imagined he deserved**

I

The Torah states:

יא. ויקח מאבני המקום וישם מראשותיו:
בראשית כח:יא

11. And he took from the stones of the place and placed them at his head.
Bereishis 28:11

Rashi comments:

And placed them at his head. He placed them in the form of a drainage channel around his head.... They began arguing with each other. Each one said, "Upon me will the righteous man rest his head...." Immediately the Holy One, blessed be He, turned them into a single stone. And that is why the verse states, "And he took the *stone* that he had placed at his head" (*Bereishis* 28:18).

The topic of the stones becoming one correlates with the meaning of Yaakov's dream. And we will begin by addressing the topic of dreams and prophecy overall.

When is a dream a complete prophecy?

The *Baal Haturim* writes that "dream" has the same *gematria* ("84") as the phrase, "That is in prophecy." Indeed the Sages state that a dream is a sixtieth of prophecy (*Berachos* 57b). However, the Sages also state that dreams are foolish and that even a true dream contains meaningless matters. How, then, did Yaakov know when he awoke that his dream was a complete prophecy?

One may suggest the following. The Sages state that the Holy One, blessed be He, does not perform a miracle without cause (see *Berachos* 58a). Therefore, the merging together of the stones had to have had a purpose, and that was to serve as a heavenly sign to Yaakov that his dream was true. And when he recognized that truth, the intensity of his awareness cast fear upon him. Therefore, states the verse, "He grew afraid, and he said, 'How awesome is this place'" (*Bereishis* 28:17).

"And he grew afraid, and he said, 'How awesome is this place"

But why did Hashem choose to perform that particular miracle? What meaning does an argument among stones have? Furthermore, what was accomplished by turning them into a single stone? If that one stone was an amalgam of the twelve stones, the portion upon which Yaakov's head rested would boast to the other parts of the stone, and strife and jealousy would continue to exist! The merging of the stones would thus have accomplished nothing!

The depth of the miracle of the unification of the twelve stones

The Midrash states:

> Rabbi Yehudah said: [Yaakov] took twelve stones. [And] the Holy One, blessed be He, decreed that he would establish the twelve tribes.
> [Yaakov] said, "Avraham did not establish them [and] Yitzchak did not establish them. If these twelve stones unite with each other, I will know that I will establish the twelve tribes." The twelve stones united with each other, and so he knew that he would establish the twelve tribes.
> *Bereishis Rabbah* 68:11.

This teaching appears with greater elaboration in *Pirkei Derebbe Eliezer*:

> Yaakov took twelve stones of the stones of the altar upon which Yitzchak, his father, had been bound [at the *Akeidah*], and he placed them at his head—which lay at that same place [his father had been bound] —to indicate to himself that twelve tribes would arise from him. And they all became one stone to inform him that all [the tribes] would be one nation on the earth. As the verse states, "Who is like Your nation Israel, one nation on the earth?" (*Chronicles* 1 17:21).
> *Pirkei Derebbe Eliezer* 35:5

We see an important insight here: these stones represented the tribes of G-d, and their unity is reflected in the unity of the nation of Israel. (We will delve deeper into this below).

When all are united, there is no jealousy and competition

When the stones were arguing and each one stated, "Upon me will the righteous man rest his head," each one was focused only on itself. But when they miraculously became one, there was no more jealousy, hatred, and competition, and no personal motives. Therefore, no matter what part of the stone Yaakov rested his head on, it was as though he rested his head on every part of it. That strengthened the unity of all Israel as "the congregation of Yaakov." And this is apparently alluded to in the term, "*meirashosav*," "at his head," whose plural grammatical form indicates two heads: the physical aspect of the head and its spiritual aspect as the site of the soul. As is known, Yaakov's soul unites the entire stature of the Congregation of Israel in order to guard it during the exile in keeping with the Sages' statement, "Just as his offspring are alive, so is he alive" (*Taanis* 5b). (See more on this below.)

Allusions in the word *avanim*, "stones"

All of this is alluded to in the word אבנים *avanim,* "stones."

Avanim may be read as אב-בנים *av-banim,* "father, children." It may also be read as א-בנים *alef-banim,* "oneness of the children," which fits beautifully with the previous explanation that the purpose of the entire episode was to bring about unity among the nation of Israel.

An expression of unity among stones to indicate the unity of the Jewish people appears also on the Kohen Gadol's breastplate, on which were set twelve stones representing the tribes of Israel, and which he wore on his heart, as the verse says,

"And they will be upon the heart of Aharon" (*Shemos* 28:30).

The unity of Israel is drawn from their faith in Hashem's oneness

The holy books state that the oneness of Israel is drawn from our faith in the oneness of Hashem. The verse states, "You have affirmed Hashem on this day, and Hashem has affirmed you on this day" (*Devarim* 26:17-18). The Sages comment on this:

> The Holy One, blessed be He, said to [the people of] Israel: You made me a single entity in the world. As the verse states, "Hear O Israel, Hashem our G-d, Hashem is one" (*Devarim* 6:4). And I will make *you* a single entity in the world. As the verse states, "And who is like Your people Israel, one nation in the world?" (*Chronicles* 1 17:21).
>
> *Chagigah* 3a

The meaning of this passage appears to be that as a result of our saying, "Hear O Israel"—which the Sages interpret as hearing with our ears what we say with our mouths, which means that we internalize the faith that Hashem is one—the Holy One, Who makes peace in His heights, will make peace for all Israel so that we will be a single entity that has no equal in the world.

The meaning of the prayer, "Guardian of Israel"

(This explains the statement found in the holy books that the evil sin of baseless hatred damages Hashem's oneness, as it were, which in turn, helps us understand why Hashem's response to this sin was to remove His Divine Presence from among us through the destruction of our Beis Hamikdash and our exile among the nations, as will be discussed below.)

Perhaps this is the meaning of the prayer, "Guardian of Israel… let [the people of] Israel, who say, 'Hear O Israel'"—thus declaring Hashem's oneness—"guard the remnant of one nation and may one nation that unifies Your name—'Hashem our G-d, Hashem is one'—not be destroyed." That is, by declaring Hashem's oneness, we maintain our own oneness. The deep connection between this prayer and the dream of Yaakov will be discussed further on.

And *Pirkei Derebbe Eliezer* (chapter 35) states: "The Holy One, blessed be He, showed [Yaakov] four kingdoms ruling and perishing. He showed him the prince of the kingdom of Bavel rising…."

Yaakov's dream showed him that which will occur to the people of Israel for the entire exile until the end of days.

Yaakov entered into darkness in order to help all of the generations in times of darkness

The *Sefas Emes* teaches:

> Yaakov Avinu surely did not need dreams. However, [he had this dream] because he put himself in a place where he could not see with a [prophetic] "clear lens" but only through a dream [in order to give encouragement to Israel in the darkness, when the countenance of G-d is hidden]. Indeed, the entire exile is likened to a dream, as the verse states, "We were like dreamers" (*Tehillim* 126:1), and the attainment of a vision at a time of darkness—darkness being referred to as a sleep—is likewise in the nature of a dream....
>
> *Sefas Emes* 5636

It is clear from these holy words that not only was Yaakov informed about the coming periods of exile but he also willingly entered the state of darkness and hiddenness of exile in order to draw the power of faith in the one G-d to his offspring, so that they would withstand the trials of the exile, which include maintaining their oneness despite their being scattered among the nations.

An explanation of the Sages' statement that Yaakov sought to reveal the end of days

The Gemara states:

Rabbi Shimon ben Lakish said:

"Yaakov summoned his sons and said, 'Gather and I will tell you'" (*Bereishis* 49:1). Yaakov sought to reveal the end of days to his sons, but the Divine Presence left him. He said, "Perhaps, heaven forbid, there was something unfit in my fathering of these children...." His sons told him, "Hear O Israel, Hashem our G-d, Hashem is one. Just as in your heart there is only one, so too in our hearts there is only one." At that moment Yaakov said, "Blessed be the name of the glory of His sovereignty forever and ever."

Pesachim 56a

One may say that when Yaakov wished to reveal the end of days to his sons, he sought to imbue them with the strength to withstand the exiles. And he chose a propitious time for doing so, because the Divine Presence is at the head of the bed of a sick person, and he wished to connect the Divine Presence to his sons as a continuation of what he had begun years earlier when he had placed his head upon the stones. But the Divine Presence left him.

Yaakov did not know why the Divine Presence did not rest upon him

Yaakov wondered if the reason the Divine Presence did not rest upon him was due to his anguish upon having seen (prophetically) four kingdoms ruling over the people of Israel. For our Sages taught that the Divine Presence does not rest upon a person when he is sad but only when he is experiencing the joy of performing a mitzvah (*Shabbos* 40b). (Similarly, the Divine Presence had not rested upon Yaakov during the entire period in which he had mourned Yosef.) Or perhaps he was saddened by the fear that his sons were cut off from their faith in the Holy One, blessed be He, and alienated from one another. Since they all stemmed from one root, any one of them could have caused the removal of the Divine Presence. To ease his mind, therefore, Yaakov's sons said to him, "Just as in your heart you only have one, so too in our hearts we only have one: we are connected to the Unique One of the world and we are one with each other." The people of Israel are thus assured that they will survive and emerge from the exile. Indeed we pray at the time of the greatest Divine favor (Shabbos at *minchah* time), which corresponds to the messianic future, "You are one and Your name is one, and who is like Your nation Israel, one nation in the land." With this prayer, we indicate that G-d's oneness is integrated into our hearts and there will thus be oneness among the people of Israel, and we will attain complete redemption. May it come quickly, in our days, amen.

II

Another miracle regarding a stone, and the construction of the house of Israel

י. ויהי כאשר ראה יעקב את רחל בת לבן אחי אמו
ואת צאן לבן אחי אמו ויגש יעקב ויגל את האבן
מעל פי הבאר וישק את צאן לבן אחי אמו:

בראשית כט:י

10. And it was that when Yaakov saw Rachel, the daughter of Lavan, the

> brother of his mother, and the flock of Lavan the brother of his mother, Yaakov approached, and he rolled the stone from the mouth of the well, and he watered the flock of Lavan, the brother of his mother.
>
> *Bereishis* 29:10

When Yaakov saw Rachel, he approached the stone and rolled it off the mouth of the well. He had not tried to do so earlier when he was with the shepherds or even after he heard that Rachel had come. Only when he actually saw Rachel did he roll the stone off. It seems that at that moment he understood that he had met his wife and had thus succeeded in his journey to the house of Lavan. This understanding gave him the strength to remove the stone. One may add that when he felt how easy it was to lift the stone, "like removing the stopper from a bottle" (Rashi on *Bereishis* 29:10), he saw his wondrous strength as a sign from heaven that this miracle involving a stone came about as an extension of the miracle of the twelve stones that had turned into one. This stone upon the well might represent the building of the construction of the nation of Israel. Yaakov easily raised the "stone," the foundation of the future nation, and he could say, "Now I will 'build' (*evneh,* the same letters as the word *ha'even*) 'the stone,' corresponding to my future twelve sons, and I will unite them into a single nation, like this single stone." Indeed, the *Baal Haturim* provides support for this approach: "**And he rolled.** When [Yaakov] saw [Rachel], the Divine Presence and Divine inspiration rested upon him."

We see two things here: First, that the moment Yaakov saw Rachel, the Divine Presence and Divine inspiration rested upon him. (Thus, Rashi states that at that time "he foresaw with Divine inspiration that [Rachel] would not be buried together with him.") From this, he knew that Rachel was a holy woman. Yaakov sensed that he was in a new and more elevated state of being, and thus he could attempt to raise the stone. One may say that Yaakov's recognition of his supernatural strength was an additional sign that he had found his wife (just as years earlier Eliezer, by means of the sign at the well, was sure that he had found Yitzchak's future wife). Thus, Yaakov was sure that Rachel was destined to be his wife and the mother of the nation of Israel.

III

A deeper look at Yaakov's proposal to marry Rachel

One may wonder how it was that Yaakov, who was a wise, understanding, and intelligent person, and who knew clearly that Lavan was dishonest, immediately proposed to work for seven years, which was an exorbitant cost? Even a Jew who is sold into slavery to repay a theft, serves no more than six years....

One may say that it was precisely because Yaakov had great intelligence and deep intentions that he made that proposal. Let us consider the chain of events: when Yaakov saw Rachel for the first time, in his great love for her he demonstrated incredible strength and rolled the stone from the mouth of the well without any help from the shepherds, and he then "raised his voice and wept." Why did he weep? Because he knew that although she was the wife designated for him by heaven, she would nevertheless not be buried with him in Ma'aras Hamachpelah.

Despite his great love for Rachel, Yaakov did not immediately tell Lavan that he wished to marry her. Rather, "he dwelt with him for a full month" (*Bereishis* 29:14) and, during that time, studied

Lavan and got to know his character, and learned the customs of the place. He knew well that Lavan would blackmail him and afterwards also cheat him, and he also learned that "it is not done so in our place to give the young one before the first-born" (ibid. 26). Yaakov's question was, how could he quickly close the deal, at least fundamentally (all the while being mindful that even after an agreement was reached, Lavan would attempt to cheat him)? His solution was to surprise Lavan with an attractive proposal that he could not refuse: seven years of service!

One might think that with this offer, Yaakov violated the prohibition of presenting an idolater with an unearned gift (based on the verse, "Do not be gracious to them" [*Devarim* 7:2]) and the prohibition of accepting enslavement to a gentile (Rambam, *Hilchos Avadim* 1:3). But that is not the case. In this regard, Yaakov learned an important lesson from Avraham. When Avraham wished to acquire Ma'aras Hamachpelah, he did not bargain. From the outset, he said, "For a full price let him give it to me" (*Bereishis* 23:9). And immediately following a hint from Ephron, "Avraham weighed for Ephron the silver that he had named in the ears of the children of Ches: 400 silver shekels, accepted by the merchant" (*Bereishis* 23:16). This is because when it comes to a mitzvah—especially a matter of important for the people of Israel—we happily pay full price. All the more so when it comes to marrying one of the Matriarchs who would build the House of Israel and especially when it comes to marrying the mainstay of the House of Israel, as even the children of Leah acknowledged regarding Rachel (see *Yalkut Shimoni,* end of *Rus*). (And indeed, the *Zohar* states that a person must pay in full for a mitzvah item in order to demonstrate the mitzvah's importance to him.)

Lavan was indeed surprised, and perhaps even stunned by Yaakov's offer. He signed the contract Yaakov wrote and obligated himself on behalf of Rachel, his youngest daughter: "And Lavan said, 'It is better that I give her to you than that I give her to another man. Dwell with me'" (*Bereishis* 29:19).

Beyond the goal of beguiling Lavan, Yaakov intended to work in a way that would subjugate only his hands and feet to Lavan, but not his spirit. First and foremost, it was Yaakov himself and not Lavan who proposed the seven years of service. His commitment was thus in accordance with his own intent, which was not to subjugate himself to a gentile but to actualize his mother's prophecy —"And you shall dwell with him for a few days" (*Bereishis* 27:44)—in order to attain Rachel.

In addition to the above, one may say that the verse stating that Yaakov's period of subservience was "in his eyes like a few days because of his love for her" (*Bereishis* 29:20) refers specifically to the first six years, because he saw that as a normative price to pay in order to fulfill the mission of building the house of Israel. As for the seventh year, with which he had beguiled Lavan, that corresponded to "on the seventh he will go free" (*Shemos* 21:2) and "a year of rest" (*Vayikra* 21:4). During that year, Yaakov already felt joyful and saw the light at the end of the tunnel. This is because the bride is given a year to outfit herself and prepare for the wedding (Rashi on *Bereishis* 24:55).

Lavan was afraid of Yaakov's physical and spiritual might

On the night of Yaakov's marriage to Rachel, Lavan exchanged Rachel with Leah. The next morning, after Yaakov discovered the deception and remonstrated with Lavan, Lavan proposed that following the week of festivities Yaakov could marry Rachel and then work for another seven years. But this is difficult to understand. If Lavan felt guilty that he substituted Leah for Rachel, why did he demand that Yaakov serve him for another seven years? And if he did not feel guilty, he should have bargained for even more years of servitude and withheld Rachel until after they were completed. Why instead did he give Rachel away immediately and also limit himself to "only" seven additional years of servitude?

Lavan knew of Yaakov's immense physical strength from the episode of Yaakov rolling the stone off the well upon arriving at Padan Aram. Lavan also came to recognize Yaakov's spiritual strength, as he was forced to admit: "I have engaged in divination and [I see that] Hashem blessed me because of you" (*Bereishis* 30:27). Therefore, now that Lavan Having violated his agreement with Yaakov, Lavan was now afraid that Yaakov would crush him with his physical and spiritual strength.

Lavan was a miser and he insisted on receiving "what he deserved"

Notwithstanding his concern for his own well-being, however, Lavan still demanded—because, in his view, it was only fair—that Yaakov work for him another seven years. Not more than seven years but also not less! He argued, "With the work that you already did, you earned Leah as your wife, though not Rachel, because 'it is not done in our place to give the younger one before the firstborn' (*Bereishis* 29:26). You have shown, however, that you regard Rachel as being worth seven years of labor. As such, when I give her to you as a wife, you will be obligated to me for seven years." As for why Lavan gave Rachel to Yaakov immediately, one may say that this is because Lavan was a miser and wanted to save the expenses of another wedding, and he made this second wedding from the leftovers of Leah's wedding.

Parashas Vayishlach

I

- **The Ramban states that all of Yaakov's deeds were for the sake of Israel for all generations**
- **"And a man wrestled with him until the break of dawn" alludes to the great struggles preceding the Redemption**
- ***Maariv* was instituted to protect us during the darkness of our exile**
- **Yaakov's steadfast Emunah for twenty-two years without Yosef and without Divine inspiration set a path for future generations to follow during our days of darkness**

- **Yaakov revealed "Hear, O Israel" specifically for the time of the darkness of exile**
- **"Regarding the remnants of the house of their scribes" (*Shemoneh Esrei*): the remnants of the Jewish people survive in the merit of Yaakov**
- **Yaakov returned for the small jugs in order to arouse salvation in every generation**

II

- **Explaining the name Ben Oni**
- **The deeper meaning of Binyamin's birth**
- **Rachel as the "Mainstay of the House"**
- **The deeper meaning of the midwife's words**
- **Rachel came back to life to see her son and name him**
- **Allusions in the name Ben Oni**

I

The Torah states:

ט. וַיֹּאמֶר אִם יָבוֹא עֵשָׂו אֶל הַמַּחֲנֶה הָאַחַת וְהִכָּהוּ וְהָיָה הַמַּחֲנֶה הַנִּשְׁאָר לִפְלֵיטָה:

בראשית לב:ט

9. And he said, "If Esav will come to the one camp and strike it, the remaining camp will be for a remnant."

Bereishis 32:9

All of Yaakov's prayers were for his time and for the future as well

In his introduction to this *parashah,* the Ramban writes that it comes to teach us that Yaakov's prayers and activities were not only for his time but for the future as well. The verse, "Hashem has rescued Yaakov and redeemed him from the hand of one stronger than he" (*Yirmiyahu* 31:10), refers not only to Hashem redeeming Yaakov in his time but also to Hashem redeeming the nation of Yaakov/Yisrael from the hand of mightier enemies in the future.

Based on these holy words of the Ramban, one may suggest that the counsel of Yaakov, "the remaining camp will be for a remnant," "והיה המחנה הנשאר לפליטה" applies in the future in the sense that his action will guard the nation of Israel for the course of all the generations to come, so that the remnant of Israel will escape from all the nations that will want to eliminate it.

Indeed, one may say that this goes beyond the Torah principle that the events the experienced by the Patriarchs serve as a paradigm for the future Jewish people ("the deed of the forefathers is a sign for the children"). For whereas in Yaakov's own time, Hashem saved him from Esav, causing Esav to not attack the camp, in the future, Hashem would save Yaakov's descendants even after they were attacked. This is in keeping with the principle that "the Holy One, blessed be He, brings about what the righteous man decrees." Yaakov's declaration of "the remaining camp will be for a remnant!" had the effect that in the coming generations there would always be a surviving remnant of Israel.

"Until the break of dawn": the purpose of the dark days of the exile is to reach until the birth pangs of the Mashiach

The verse says, "And a man wrestled with him until the break of dawn" (*Bereishis* 32:10). This may be interpreted as teaching that throughout the course of that night – i.e., "until the break of dawn" (which alludes to exile) – Yaakov fought for the sake of his children (i.e., until the dawn of the Redemption). Then, as the *piyut* states, "The dark of the night will shine like the light of the day." Indeed, commentators have pointed out that in the verse, "Then your light will break forth as the dawn" (*Yeshayahu* 58:8), which refers to the Redemption, the Hebrew word "*yibaka,*" "break forth," consists of the letters that spell "Yaakov." That is, the light of Redemption comes in the merit of Yaakov's statement/action, which was effectively a decree: "And the remaining camp will escape" (*Bereishis* 32:9).

We are prohibited from eating the sciatic nerve because "the socket of Yaakov's hip became dislocated as he wrestled with him" (*Bereishis* 32:26; see ibid. 33). This injury was inflicted on Yaakov at the end of the night, after which the angel asked Yaakov to send him away, "because the dawn is breaking" (*Bereishis* 32:26). There is a powerful and wondrous allusion here: As the era of the Redemption approaches, the suffering of the Jewish people will increase. Just as birth pangs grow progressively stronger just before the miracle of birth, so too the birth pangs of Mashiach will grow progressively stronger before the Redemption. And these birth pangs are alluded to by the dislocation of Yaakov's hipbone and his limping on his thigh at the end of his struggle just as dawn approached.

Yaakov instituted *maariv* to guard us in the exile, which is like the night

Accordingly, we may understand why Yaakov instituted *maariv,* which takes place at night. This is because in the night—i.e., the exile—he prays on behalf of all generations and illuminates a way for us to be rescued from all who wish to destroy us.

The Sages derive that Yaakov instituted the prayer of *maariv* from the verse, "He came upon the place, and he lodged there, because the sun had set" (*Bereishis* 28:11, *Berachos* 26b). Commenting on this verse, the Midrash (see *Torah Sheleimah,* p. 1124) states that the Divine inspiration rested on him there, and he prophesied that the people of Israel would sin and as a result Divine inspiration would leave them. These two ideas—i.e., Yaakov instituting *maariv,* and his prophesying that the Divine presence would leave the Children of Israel, must therefore be linked: since Yaakov saw the darkness descending upon his children, he instituted *maariv* to shield and protect them.

Yaakov's prayer guards us during the exile, which is compared to the night. Thus, the blessing of *hashkiveinu* in the *maariv* liturgy ends with the words, "He Who guards His nation Israel forever," because Hashem's continuous protection of the Jewish people is in the merit of Yaakov.

The twenty-two-year period in which Yosef was missing and Yaakov remained a believer gives us faith until this very day

For twenty-two years, Yosef was missing, and Yaakov was without Divine inspiration, yet Yaakov did not lose his faith. One may say that this constituted a paradigm and a source of empowerment for us to stand firm in our own faith after the disappearance of prophecy and Divine inspiration during periods of exile. When Yaakov descended to the Egyptian exile, which is the root of all the exiles, the Divine Presence accompanied him there to protect Israel for generations to come, in keeping with the Sages' statement, "When Israel was exiled, the Divine Presence was exiled." The way he brought all of that about was by accepting Hashem's assurance, "I will descend with you to Egypt, and I will also bring you up" (*Bereishis* 46:4).

In the midst of the Egyptian exile, before Yaakov passed away, he asked Hashem to reveal the end in order to strengthen us. Although that knowledge was denied him, he nevertheless bequeathed to us the *Sh'ma,* which is the foundation of our faith and maintains us to the end of all generations: ‘"Hear O Israel, Hashem our G-d, Hashem is one.’ Just as in your heart there is only one, so too in our hearts there is only one.’" That is to say, everything is in Yaakov’s merit, and through him we maintain our hope: "Guard the remnant of Israel and do not destroy the [children of] Israel, who say, ‘Hear O Israel."

Moreover, the Guardian of Israel will not only rescue us, but He will elevate the glory of Israel. Throughout all the years of exile, not only have the children of Israel been revived and awakened from the dust of evil decrees and destruction, but they have gained strength they did not possess prior to the decree, and the periods of darkness they endured have been followed by the great light of Torah that illuminates the entire world with new Torah insights for all the coming generations.

Great Torah figures who lost everything but arose to bring about the renaissance of the Jewish people

An outstanding example of this rising up from the dust and ashes was the holy Admor of Sanz-Klausenberg, who lost everything in the Shoah and who, upon emerging from the valley of tears, a brand plucked from fire, became father and mother to the orphans of that generation. From the first Yom Kippur after the liberation in the Foehrenwald DP camp and onward, he established upright generations, with institutions such as the yeshiva he called She'eris Hapleita and the well-known Laniado Hospital in Kiryat Sanz. Indeed, he built an entire world of Torah and Hasidism.

The Klausenberger Rebbe's strength to do what he did came from Yaakov's blessing and prayer that in every generation there should be a camp that remains as a remnant, and which, moreover, receives extraordinary abilities to bring about rectification and intensify the presence of Hashem and the influence of His Torah.

In Yaakov's merit, there will always be a "surviving camp"

The above is alluded to in the prayer, "And upon the remnant of the house of their scribes" (*Shemoneh Esrei*). The assurance that "there will be a camp remaining as a remnant" exists specifically in "the house of their scribes"—that is, in the shuls and *batei midrashos*. As the verse states, "How goodly are your tents, O Yaakov, your dwelling places, Israel" (*Bamidbar* 24:5). This refers to the blessing that shuls and *batei midrashos* will always exist, an eternal blessing that will never be transformed into a curse (*Sanhedrin* 105b).

This may be part of the meaning of the Sages' statement, "Yaakov Avinu did not die—just as his offspring are alive, so is he alive" (*Taanis* 5b). For, what merit did Yaakov's offspring have that they remained alive and survived all the difficult exiles? It was the merit of Yaakov's above-mentioned prayer, a prayer he still engages in on our behalf. "And the remaining camp will be for a remnant" is Yaakov's perpetual prayer, enduring for all time.

Yaakov returned for the small jugs; as a result, Hashem's salvation will be available in every generation

The verse says, "Yaakov remained alone." Rashi states, "He had forgotten small jugs and returned for them" (*Bereishis* 32:25). The midrashim state that because Yaakov returned for these small jugs, we gained the jug of oil of the Chanukah miracle. Yaakov returned for jug*s,* in the plural (see *Bnei Yissachar, Chanukah* 10). Yaakov saw from afar all the troubles that would befall Israel throughout the course of the generations, and he saw that they would require many miracles. He thus returned for the small jugs, thereby actuating a miraculous power for all the times in which Israel would require miraculous salvation.

Thus is the verse, "Hashem has redeemed Yaakov and rescued him from the hand of one stronger than he" (*Yirmiyahu* 31:10) realized in Yaakov's children. Blessed are You, Hashem, Who has rescued Israel. And may that rescue be complete, quickly, in our days, amen.

II

Explaining the name Ben Oni

וַיְהִי בְהַקְשֹׁתָהּ בְּלִדְתָּהּ וַתֹּאמֶר לָהּ הַמְיַלֶּדֶת אַל תִּירְאִי כִּי גַם זֶה לָךְ בֵּן:

וַיְהִי בְּצֵאת נַפְשָׁהּ כִּי מֵתָה וַתִּקְרָא שְׁמוֹ בֶּן אוֹנִי וְאָבִיו קָרָא לוֹ בִנְיָמִין:

"And it came to pass, when she was in hard labor, that the midwife said unto her: 'Fear not; for this also is a son for you. And it came to pass, as her soul was in departing--for she died--she called his name Ben-oni; but his father called him Binyamin." (*Bereshis* 35, 17-18)

There is much that needs to be explained in these two short *pesukim*.

What was Rachel afraid of?

How did the midwife telling her "this also is a son for you" calm her?

Why the repetition of "as her soul was in departing--for she died"?

According to the continuation of the *pasuk* it appears that Rachel named her son after she died. How is that possible?

Why did the Torah mention that Rachel named him "Ben Oni"? This is difficult to understand for two reasons:

A. His real, and used name is Binyamin, as is evident in all of the Torah and by how our Sages refer to him.

B. Even worse, it seems as though the righteous Rachel *Imeinu* (our matriarch) was upset over his birth, G-d forbid, as "Ben Oni" ***seemingly*** translates as "son of my affliction".

The deeper meaning of Binyamin's birth

With of Binyamin's birth four things took place - two for Rachel and two for the Jewish nation.

For Rachel - She not only died following Binyamin's birth, but because she died at that time, "on the road to Efrat", and she was buried there, and not in *Me'arat HaMachpela* together with Yaakov.

For the Jewish nation - Beyond the addition of a tribe, in whose share Beit Hamikdash will be built, the Jewish nation is also now complete, **since with the birth of Binyamin, we have now all 12 tribes that were destinated to be born and the nation is now complete and unified** through all 12 tribes, and the *Sechina* of G-d, who is One in the world, and dwells among them when they are together and unified. Now they are the "**nation of oneness**" (גוי אחד). **The numerical value of אחד** (one) **is 13 - the 12 tribes plus G-d, who is one.**

Rachel as the "Mainstay of the House"

All these aspects are strongly connected to each other in a way that cannot be severed. Rachel *imeinu* is a symbol of devotion and self-sacrifice for others in general, and especially for the Jewish nation. Her entire desire was to have the tribes and protect them, even at significant costs: to die in order to have the tribe of Binyamin, to complete the Jewish nation, and be buried "on the way", and not in *Me'arat Hamachpela,* to be able to evoke ***rachamim* – a mother's mercy** (see first entry in Chayei Sarah) for her children as they head to exile.

The only fear Rachel had was that, G-d forbid, she would be unable to fulfill her destiny and have at least two tribes. She did not want to be less than the maids. That was her entire desire and goal. Even at the birth of Yosef, she immediately included a prayer in his name: "And she named him Yosef saying, may G-d **add (*Yosef*)** me another **son**". Rashi comments: "She knew through prophesy that Yaakov will only have 12 tribes. She said, may it be G-d will, that the last tribe will be from me, and that's why she asked for another **son**". (*Bereshis* 30, 24 and Rashi there). She was afraid she would not merit to complete the Jewish nation and not be "**The Mainstay of the House** [of the Jewish people]" with the responsibility to pray for, and protect, the Jewish nation - and she will G-d forbid, die without fulfilling her destiny.

The deeper meaning of the midwife's words

And that's why the midwife told her "Fear not" - meaning, whatever you go through, whatever happens, it will not be in vain. "For this also is a **son**" - meaning, you fulfilled your destiny and got to have not only another tribe but גם ז"ה, the numeric value of **זה** is 12. **The merit for completing the 12 tribes is yours**. Through this son, everything that will happen to you will not be in vain, for you merited completing and ensuring the eternal existence of the Jewish nation!

Rachel came back to life to see her son and name him

"And it came to pass, as her soul was departing--for she died" - we see in the midrash that the repetition is to emphasize that she was really dead and completely sacrificed herself to have Binyamin and complete the Jewish nation. In my humble opinion, as a merit of her sacrifice **she momentarily came back to life** so that hearing the news in the world to come, would not be greater than seeing for herself in this world, **to see and make a blessing for what she accomplished**. Moreover, by seeing Binyamin herself in this world, **as a mother**, she is filled with ***rachamim*** over her son and all the Jewish nation that he completed, and so in the future she will pray from the bottom of her heart, **a mother's heart**, as it says: "**Rachel is weeping for her children**." (Yirmiyahu 31,14).

Allusions in the name Ben Oni

Based on what we wrote, we can suggest "she called his name **Ben-oni**", simply means that she got to see him and say "**for him I labored, and worked hard, and sacrificed**". We can also suggest that the meaning of ***oni*** is my **strength**, as we see with Yaakov: "Reuven, you are my first-born, my might, and ראשית **אוני** - first of **my strength**..." (*Bereishis* 49, 3). Binyamin is the **last** of Yaakov and **Rachel's strength**, a favorite last, as Binyamin completed the Jewish nation. Rachel is giving a blessing saying: "**This is my strength! Through this son I have reached the status of "Mainstay of the House** [of Israel]" **and I fulfilled my role to**

establish the Jewish nation and, in the future, pray for them to ensure their future redemption".

It occurred to me that it is hinted at in the Hebrew word Oni, **אונ"י**, with a reduced numerical value is **13**, that through this son I completed the **גי' אח"ד** - the **12** tribes plus the value of **unity**, in present and in the future, through my prayer.

Parashas Vayeishev - Chanukah

I

- **An explanation of the statement that Hashem "performed miracles for our fathers in those days at this time" (siddur)**
- **The Holy One, blessed be He, continues to this day to perform miracles for us**
- **If a person forgot to say "Al Hanisim," he can say, "May the Compassionate One do miracles *for us...*"**
- **Why did Yaakov display an exceptional love for Yosef?**
- **An explanation of the "Yehi Ratzon" prayer preceding "Birkas Kohanim" on the holidays**
- **Yosef's striped coat corresponds to the clothes of the Kohanim**
- **"Israel loved" means that he had exceptional compassion for Yosef**
- **A number of matters that are discussed specifically on *daf* 22 of Tractate *Shabbos***

II

- **What is the meaning of "this" in "this dream"?**
- **A special dream that foreshadows all that will happen to the nation of Israel**
- **Which dream did Yosef tell his father about and which did he not tell him about?**
- **Yosef did not tell his father about the dream that his brothers interpreted for the good**

III

- **"His father guarded the matter" (*Bereishis* 37:11) means that he looked forward to its realization**
- **In the merit of Yaakov and Yosef learning about the *eglah arufah*, Yosef was rescued from his brothers**

IV

- **An explanation of the adjacency of two teachings of Rabbi Tanchum**
- **From the laws of Chanukah, we see the people of Israel's devotion to the mitzvos**
- ***Mehadrin min hamehadrin* expresses the people of Israel's love for acting in purity**
- **Supernatural miracles show Hashem's love for us, measure for measure**

V

- **Moshe had difficulty understanding how the menorah was to be constructed**
- **A midrashic explanation of this**
- **In precisely the area in which Moshe had difficulty, the great light of Chanukah emerged**

I

The meaning of "in those days, at this time"

When we light the Chanukah candles, we recite the blessing, "Who did miracles for our forefathers in those days, at this time." Also when we say "Al Hanisim," we state, "that You did for our forefathers in those days, at this time." Great rabbis have addressed "at this time" to mean "during this season" (Kislev).

As the son of a Holocaust survivors, when I light the Chanukah candles, I feel that it is an incomparably and immeasurably deep matter. It is similar to the prayer of thanks that we recite every day "for Your miracles every day with us"—i.e., for the miracles of "those days" that the Hashem continues to do for us "at this time."

Indeed, this is in accordance with the view of the *Baal Halevushim* that

we thank Hashem for the miracles He did for our forefathers in those days, **and** we also thank Him for the revealed and hidden miracles that He does for us at this time.

נוסח הלבוש: בימים ההם ובזמן הזה

If a person forgot to say "Al Hanisim," he can say, "May the Compassionate One do miracles for us..."

If a person forgot to say "Al Hanisim," he can say, "May the Compassionate One do miracles for us as He did for our forefathers...." In this way, he expresses our request that Hashem draw the power of these miracles upon us at present. For indeed these miracles continue and have assisted us throughout. As the Yaavetz states in his commentary on the siddur, the fact that the people of Israel have survived all of the difficult times of oppression and persecution is the greatest of all miracles.

The Sages state (*Shabbos* 22b) that the westernmost lamp of the menorah gave testimony that the Divine Presence rests among the people of Israel (because it miraculously always burned longer than the other lamps, despite having the same amount of oil as the other lamps). And the Chanukah lights, which are a reflection of the menorah, testify that when the Divine Presence rests upon the nation of Israel they will illuminate the world.

Why Yaakov "loved Yosef more than [he did] all his brothers"

The Torah states that "Israel loved Yosef more than [he did] all his brothers" (*Bereishis* 37:3). It is surprising that Yaakov showed more love to one of his sons than to his other sons, a factor that led to jealousy and hatred. And also, why did Yaakov give specifically a striped coat to Yosef?

In the "*Yehi Ratzon*" prayer recited after the "Birkas Kohanim" in *Musaf* on the holidays, we say, "Grant us grace and kindness and compassion in Your eyes and in the eyes of all who see us, just as You granted Yosef Your righteous one when his father clothed him with a striped coat for grace and kindness and compassion in Your eyes and in the eyes of all who saw him." But that is surprising, since apparently the striped coat led to jealousy and hatred, and not to finding grace in the eyes of those who saw him. And besides that, what is the connection between this and "Birkas Kohanim"?

An explanation of the prayer recited at the time of "Birkas Kohanim" on the holidays

Possibly Yaakov did not externally display extra love for Yosef. Indeed, when Yosef related his dream, "his father rebuked him ... 'Will we truly come, I and your mother and your brothers, to bow before you to the ground?" (*Bereishis* 37:10). Rashi explains that with these words, Yaakov was rebuking Yosef "because he brought hostility upon himself."

The Torah states that "Israel loved Yosef more than [he did] all his brothers," and thus gave Yosef a striped coat. The verse uses the name "Israel" and not "Yaakov." The name "Israel" corresponds to the measure of the nation of Israel, and when this measure or reference to the nation is present, there is no hatred (as explained earlier with regard to "When the stones were arguing and each one stated, "Upon me shall the righteous man place his head," that when they are all unified into one entity -one stone- there is no jealousy among its components). See Parshas Vayeitzei.

Yosef's striped coat corresponded to the garments of the Kohanim

Yosef's striped coat corresponded to the garments of the Kohanim. Yaakov had acquired the firstborn status from Esav, and before the sin of the Golden Calf, the firstborn fulfilled the role of the Kohen. Reuven was Yaakov's firstborn son from Leah, but he lost his firstborn status when he disordered his father's bed (*Bereishis* 35:22), and it passed to Yosef, Yaakov's firstborn son from Rachel. This is why no Israelite is jealous of a Kohen or Levi –

because it is necessary for there to be Kohanim, Levi'im and Yisraelim. The verse thus associates the striped coat with the name "Israel," which corresponds to the nation of Israel, because on that level no one is jealous of anyone else.

In this regard, the *Kli Yakar* teaches:

> "And he made him a striped coat." Reuven had already disordered his father's bed, [so] the firstborn status was taken away from him. [Yaakov] now transferred it to Yosef. In this regard, Yaakov made Yosef a striped coat, because the service was performed by the firstborn, and the firstborn was "kohen to the supernal G-d." Therefore, [Yaakov] made this coat for honor and splendor, similar to the "coat of checker work" [of the priestly garments] (*Shemos* 28:4).

Similarly, Rabbeinu Bachaye writes that the Kohen's "coat of checker work" corresponds to Yosef's striped coat.

"Israel loved Yosef" means that he had compassion on Yosef

Furthermore, one may say that "Israel loved Yosef" means that Yaakov had compassion for Yosef (cf. Onkelos).

Prior to Yosef's birth, Yaakov had undergone many trials and tribulations. First, he served Lavan for seven years so he would be able to marry Rachel and Yosef would be his firstborn. But Lavan deceived him and gave him Leah. When he finally did marry Rachel, she was infertile, and only in his later years did he father Yosef, who attained the firstborn status.

Yaakov thus had so much compassion for Yosef because Yosef had been born after Yaakov had undergone many tribulations.

This explains the connection with "Birkas Kohanim," because when Israel (a name associated with oneness of the Jewish people) clothed Yosef in the striped coat, Yosef became a Kohen. And with that, he received grace and kindness "in the eyes of all who saw him," who, as "one nation," recognized the need for a Kohen. And that protected Yosef: Hashem would perform miracles to guard him against all the evils and dangers that he would face.

All of these matters are alluded to in Tractate *Shabbos*, p. 22

The Sages state teach that "a person should always look forward to [fulfillment of a] good dream up to twenty-two years [after the dream]" (*Berachos* 55b), just as Yosef's dream was realized only at twenty-two years. Three related concepts appear in Tractate *Shabbos* on p. 22: "The pit was empty, it contained no water in it" (*Bereishis* 37:24): the empty pit that was deeper than twenty cubits; the menorah as testimony that the Divine Presence rests among Israel; and an allusion to Yosef's dream and its interpretation (as will be discussed below).

In Yosef's statement, "Now hear this dream that I dreamed..." (*Bereishis* 37:6), the use of "*this* dream" is not as colloquial as "the dream." The same is true of Yaakov's statement, "What is *this* dream that you have dreamed?" (*Bereishis* 37:10). As is known, however, the word "this" refers to something explicit and revealed. What, then, was explicit and revealed in Yosef's dreams?

II

"*This* dream" - i.e., a special dream

Yaakov had previously said, "Indeed, Hashem is in *this* place" (*Bereishis* 28:16). The word "this" indicates that the place was uniquely suited for the revelation of the Divine Presence. Similarly, at the Red Sea, the children of Israel sang, "*This* is my G-d, and I will glorify Him" (*Shemos* 15:2). Indeed, the Divine Presence was revealed there at that time. "*This* dream" may thus may indicate a dream that is special insofar as it explicitly reveals Divine inspiration. And since that is how Yosef and Yaakov understood Yosef's dream, they referred to it as "*this* dream." And since Yaakov understood the dream this way, he "guarded the matter" (*Bereishis* 37:11).

Yosef's dreams and whom he told them to

However, further explanation is required:

Regarding the first dream, it says, "Yosef dreamed a dream and told it to his brothers, and they hated him even more" (*Bereishis* 37:5). Regarding the second dream, it says, "He dreamed another dream and he told it to his brothers" (*Bereishis* 37:9), and afterward, "He told his father and his brothers, and his father rebuked him..."

(*Bereishis* 37:10). Rashi explains, "After he told it to his brothers, he went and told it to his father in their presence."

This raises several difficulties. First, why did Yosef tell his dreams at all? Was his intent to boast and denigrate his brothers? Second, why didn't he tell his father the first dream? Finally, why did Yosef tell the second dream to his brothers twice, once directly, and once when he repeated the dream in their father's presence?

Regarding the first question, Yosef did not intend to boast or denigrate his brothers. Rather, he simply wanted to know what his dreams meant. And indeed, his brothers interpreted his first dream positively: that he would become a leader. Nevertheless, after he told them the dream, they "hated him even more."

Yosef had no reason to tell his father the dream that his brothers had already interpreted

This idea is in accordance with the view of the *Sifsei Chachamim,* whose words shed light on the entire topic:

> One may say, Yosef knew that most dreams follow the interpretation given

them. And since his brothers had given a positive interpreted [to his dream], he did not want to tell it to his father. But his brothers did not interpret the second dream for him. That was because they did not want to interpret it for the good, because they too sensed that he told [them] his dreams so that they would interpret [them] for the good. Therefore, he had to tell it to his father to interpret it as he did. And [his father] rebuked him so that his brothers would not hate him.

In order to make peace, Yaakov wanted to hear the dream a second time

One may say that Yaakov had heard about the dream from Yosef's brothers, and he specifically required Yosef to relate it to him in the presence of his brothers, so that Yaakov could rebuke Yosef and contradict the dream in his brothers' presence and in this way make peace between Yosef and his brothers.

III

Davar ("matter, "word") alludes to the realization of the dreams

The word "*davar*" that appears in this narrative has two meanings: "word" and "thing."

The Torah states here, "His brothers were jealous of him, and his father guarded the matter [*davar*]" (*Bereishis* 37:11)

Rashi explains "his father guarded the matter" as meaning that Yaakov looked forward to seeing the dream come true. (The word "guard" has the meaning of "looking forward" in other verses as well, such as "guarding awaiting the realization [of G-d's promise]" (*Yishayahu* 26:2) and "You do not guard wait for my sin" (*Iyov* 14:16). Thus, when Yaakov told Yosef, "Go see to the welfare of your brothers ... and bring me back word [*davar*]..." (*Bereishis* 37:14), he hoped that Yosef would make peace with his brothers and come back to tell him as much, and this would begin the process of the realization of Yosef's dreams.

But the fulfillment of this matter [*davar*], came true only after twenty-two years.

ז. וידברו אליו את כל **דברי** יוסף אשר **דבר** אלהם וירא את העגלות אשר שלח יוסף לשאת אתו ותחי רוח יעקב אביהם.

בראשית מ"ה:כ"ז

27. They told him all of Yosef's words that he had spoken with them, and he saw the carriages that Yosef had sent to carry him, and the spirit of Yaakov their father was revived (*Bereishis* 45:27).

Rashi explains:

[Yosef] gave [his brothers] a sign of what [he and his father] had been studying when [Yosef] had left him: the topic of the *eglah arufah,* the "heifer that is to be beheaded" (*Devarim* 21). [The Hebrew for "carriage," *agalah,* is reminiscent of the Hebrew for "heifer," *eglah*.]

Now, after twenty-two years, that which Yaakov had hoped for had been realized.

Yaakov and Yosef's learning about *eglah arufah* helped rescue Yosef from his brothers

The law of *eglah arufah* pertains to situations where a person who has been killed is found in an open field. The elders of the nearest town engage in a ceremony involving the decapitation of a calf, while requesting of Hashem, "Grant atonement to Your people Israel..., and do not lay [the guilt of] innocent blood among Your nation Israel" (*Devarim* 21:8).

Perhaps it was not by happenstance that Yaakov and Yosef had learned the laws of the *eglah arufah* immediately prior to the sale of Yosef: The two are connected in that Yosef's brothers, upon returning to their father, pretended that Yosef had been slain in a field. Having dipped his coat in blood, they displayed it to their father and said, "Now recognize whether this is your son's coat" (*Bereishis* 37:32). Yaakov believed them, saying, "Indeed, Yosef has been torn apart" (*Bereishis* 37:33).

One may say that in the merit of Yaakov and Yosef learning the laws of the *eglah arufah*, Yosef was rescued from his brothers' scheme to kill him and eventually prevailed.

IV

The connection between Chanukah and *Parashas Vayeishev*

Rav Kahane said: "Rav Nosson bar Minyumi taught in the name of Rabbe Tanchum: A Chanukah menorah placed higher than twenty cubits is unkosher, similar to a sukkah and a [horizontal beam across the entrance of an] alleyway (a *mavoi*), [which makes carrying in the area on Shabbos permissible].;"

Rav Kahane also said: "Rav Nosson bar Minyumi taught in the name of Rav Tanchum: 'What is the meaning of the verse, "The pit was empty, it contained no water in it" (*Bereishis* 37:24)? Since "the pit was empty," don't I already know that it contained no water? Why, then, does the Torah tell us that "it contained no water"? [The answer is], it comes to teach us that although it contained no water, it did contain snakes and scorpions'" (*Shabbos* 21b-22a).

Over the generations, various commentators have discussed the meaning of these two teachings following one another. They say the fact that they are both by the same rabbis (i.e., Rav Kahana in the name of Rav Nosson bar Minyumi) is not a sufficient answer. However, the fact that *Parashas Vayeishev,* which contains the verse about the pit being empty, and Chanukah always fall out on dates that are close to each other (indeed sometimes *Parashas Vayeishev* occurs on Shabbos Chanukah itself) is significant.

The adjacency of these two statements of Rav Tanchum

It is forbidden to place the Chanukah menorah higher than twenty cubits because the eye does not naturally look up that high, and there is thus no publicizing of the miracle, which is an essential component of the mitzvah. Similarly, because the brothers threw Yosef into a pit deeper than twenty cubits, they could not see the great miracle of his being safe from the snakes and scorpions it contained. That too holds an encouraging message – that the Holy One, blessed be He, performs many hidden miracles on our behalf.

Incidentally, one may mention another hidden miracle that eased Yosef's suffering: in contrast to the noisome crude oil and tar that Arabs typically carried, the caravan of the Ishmaelites who bought Yosef was carrying sweet-smelling spices, balm, and lotus (*Bereishis* 37:25).

The unique structure of the laws of Chanukah mirrors the Maccabees' dedication to lighting the menorah in the most beautiful way possible

The laws of lighting the Chanukah menorah are unique in that there is a three-tier level of beautifying the mitzvah. The basic halachah is that one candle is lit for the entire family each night. The second level—*mehadrin*—is that each family member lights a candle every day. The third level—*mehadrin min hamehadrin*—is that each family member adds an additional candle every night. This reflects the fact that the people of Israel, after the Chanukah victory, dedicated themselves to lighting the menorah in the Beis Hamikdash in the most beautiful way (i.e., to lighting the wick with ritually pure oil even though they could have relied on a leniency and used ritually impure oil).

(*Beis Halevi al HaTorah* on Chanukah provides another explanation of how the Jews at that time beautified the mitzvah of lighting the Menorah in the Beis Hamikdash. He says, they could have used fine wicks, which would have allowed the oil to burn for eight days in natural manner; instead, they used thicker wicks, which produced brighter flames, in order to perform the mitzvah beautifully.) When a person dedicates himself to Hashem in a beautiful manner, Hashem behaves toward in that person in a similar manner, measure for measure, and rescues that righteous person in a beautiful manner. Thus, Hashem saves Yosef Hatzadik in miraculous ways and transports him in a sweet sweet-smelling environment and miraculously elevates him to greatness to illuminate us in our exile.

The menorah corresponds to the Divine Presence resting upon Israel

The passage in the Gemara quoted above (*Shabbos* 22b) continues:

> The verse states, "Outside the dividing curtain of the testimony, [Aharon] will arrange [the menorah]" (*Vayikra* 24:3). But does [G-d] need [the menorah's] light? After all, isn't it true that throughout the forty years the children of Israel traveled in the desert, they

traveled only by His light? Rather, [the lighting of the menorah] is testimony to humanity that the Divine Presence rests upon [the people of] Israel.
What is the [nature of this] testimony?

Rav said: "This is [expressed in] the westernmost lamp. [Aharon] would put the same amount of oil in it as in the other lamps, and he would light [the other candles] from it, and he would conclude with it—[i.e., it outlasted the other lamps]."

It appears to me that this sheds light on the following midrash:

"Hammered work [*miksheh*] of gold" (*Bamidbar* 8:4). What was the difficulty [*kasheh*] in making [the menorah] that caused Moshe to toil so much?

[But] as a result of it being difficult for Moshe, the Holy One, blessed be He, told him, "Take a talent of gold and cast it into the fire. [Then] take it out, and it will have been made by itself."

Thus does the verse state, "Its cups, its buttons, and its blossoms will be from it" (*Shemos* 25:31). It was struck with a hammer, and it was made of itself.

Therefore, [the verse] says, "It *shall be made* a hammered work" in the passive tense, indicating that it was made of itself. Moshe took the talent and cast it into the fire. Moshe said, "Master of the universe, here is a talent in the fire. As You wish, so may You do." Immediately, the menorah emerged, properly made. Therefore, the verse states, "Like the image that Hashem showed Moshe, did he make the Menorah." The verse does not state, "So did Moshe do," but "So it was made." Who did? The Holy One, blessed be He.

Midrash Rabbah, Parashas Behaaloschah 15:4

V

First Moshe toiled, and only then did the Holy One, blessed be He, make the menorah

The *Chiddushei Harim* and the *Sefas Emes* teach that this is related to the Sages' teaching that if someone states that he has toiled and found what he sought, he is to be believed. At first glance, the teaching is puzzling, because if the person toiled, then how can his achievement be described as a "find'—it is attainment. After all, finding something does not require any toil!? The *Chiddushei Harim* and *Sefas Emes* explain that we are obligated to toil in learning Torah and in performing mitzvos, but the understanding and success come to us only from Hashem; thus, it is likened to something that is found.

Why is this idea expressed particularly in the making of the menorah? Because the menorah is the testimony that the Divine Presence rests on the people of Israel; the way it is made thus demonstrates the partnership between the Jewish people and Hashem: the people of Israel *toil* to make the menorah, and the Holy One, blessed be He, Himself makes it. Moshe exerts all his effort, and Hashem enables him to complete it with divine intervention.

In accordance with this, we can understand why the Maccabees insisted on lighting the menorah in a beautiful fashion (i.e., using only ritually pure oil and thick wicks). Their doing so impelled Hashem, as it were, to make a miracle. And today as well, we perform the mitzvah of lighting the menorah in the most beautiful way possible as our way of testifying that the Divine Presence rests upon the people of Israel.

Parashas Mikeitz-Chanukah

- **The laws of Chanukah are alluded to on page 22 of Tractate *Shabbos***
- **The principal discussion there is the topic of treating a mitzvah with disdain**
- **A contradiction exists between tractate *Shabbos* and "Haneiros Halalu"; it is reconciled by the Ramban in his *Mitcham's Hashem***
- **It is forbidden to make use of the Chanukah light because it is like *hikes* (property consecrated to the Beis Hamikdash)**
- **The principal discussion about treating a mitzvah with disdain relates to Chanukah**

- **Rav Yosef initially had the characteristic of being like "Sinai," and then attained the characteristic of being an "uprooter of mountains"**
- **The connection between treating a mitzvah with disdain and an elder who forgot his learning**

The laws of Chanukah are alluded to on page 22 of Masechte *Shabbos*

As noted earlier, *Shabbos* 22 deals with the topic of Chanukah.

Shabbos 22a teaches that a menorah situated higher than twenty cubits is unkosher (similar to a sukkah and a *mavoi* that are over twenty cubits high). Rashi explains that this is because a person doesn't naturally look up that high, and thus a menorah at that height does not fulfill the purpose of publicizing the miracle of Chanukah.

This is followed by a teaching regarding the sale of Yosef, an episode that appears in the *parashah* we read in shul before or on Chanukah. (The Gemara teaches that the verse stating that Yosef was cast into a pit "that was empty—it had no water in it" [*Bereishis* 37:24] indicates that although it had no water, it did have snakes and scorpions.)

This all appears on page 22. The number twenty-two alludes to Yosef and his dream, which came true after twenty-two years. (More such associations are noted below.)

Shabbos 22b quotes the verse, "Outside the veil of testimony, he will set up [the menorah]" (*Vayikra* 24:3), and asks:

> Does [G-d] need the [menorah's] light? [Of course not!] For the entire 40 years [that the children of Israel wandered] in the desert, they proceeded only by His light.

The Gemara explains:

> [The light of the menorah] testifies to humanity that the Divine Presence rests upon Israel at all times and at every moment, constantly.

The Gemara goes on to say that the testimony lies in the miracle associated with the western light of the menorah in the Beis Hamikdash, which was used to light the other six lights of the menorah: Although its own oil would be partially consumed in the process, which took some time, the western light nevertheless outlasted the other lights.

The topic of treating a mitzvah with disdain

The principal topic discussed on page 22 of Tractate *Shabbos* is that we may not treat a mitzvah with disdain. The Gemara states:

Rav Yehudah said in the name of Rav Assi in the name of Rav:

"It is forbidden to count money opposite the Chanukah candle."

When I, [Rav Yehudah,] reported this to Shmuel, he said to me: Does [that] candle possess holiness וכי נר קדושה יש בה - , [which would prohibit a person from using its light? It doesn't, so why can't one use its light to count money?]"

Rav Yosef strongly objected to [Shmuel's question]: "And does the blood [of a slaughtered undomesticated animal or fowl] have holiness? [It doesn't, yet it still may not be treated with disdain]. For we learned in a baraisa: the verse, 'He will spill its blood ... and cover it [with dust]' (*Vayikra* 17:13) [means], with that which he spilled [the blood], he shall cover [the blood]. [Just as a person spills the blood of a slaughtered animal with his hand, so must he cover its blood with his hand]; he must not cover it with his foot, so as not to treat mitzvahs with disdain.

"Here as well, [a person may not count money opposite the Chanukah menorah] so as not to treat the mitzvos with disdain."

The Gemara thus concludes that the menorah lights are not holy and that the reason one may not make use of them to count money is so as not to treat the mitzvah with disdain.

Yet our ancient and holy text of "Haneiros Halalu," however (as recorded in *Maseches Sofrim*), does ascribe holiness to the Chanukah candles, stating:

> During all eight days of Chanukah, these candles are holy, and we do not have permission to use them, but only to see them....
>
> הנרות הללו קודש הם

How can this contradiction be explained?

The contradiction between tractate *Shabbos* and "Haneiros Halalu" is reconciled by the Ramban in his *Milchamos Hashem*

This contradiction is addressed and reconciled by the Ramban in his *Milchamos Hashem*:

> [Shmuel's] disagreement relates only to counting money [opposite the Chanukah candle], because this does not constitute "utilization" [of the light] but merely "benefiting" from it. Therefore, he said, "And does [that] candle possess holiness?" [Meaning:] Are mitzvos an object of holiness, comparable to tefillin and a Torah scroll and their accessories, from which one may not derive mundane benefit?
>
> In keeping with that, Rav Yosef said to him: "Does the blood [of a slaughtered animal] have holiness, such that a person may not treat it as he wishes? [In fact], isn't it true that mitzvah objects may [even] be discarded [after they've been used for the mitzvah]? Nevertheless, although they may be

discarded after [the performance of] the mitzvah, at the time of [the performance of] their mitzvah, we treat them as holy so that mitzvos will not be disdained. Here too, we treat [the candles] during the time of [the mitzvah] as holy objects, forbidden for mundane usages at the time of [the performance of] the mitzvah.

Rav Yosef, then, does not distinguish between the disdain [shown by counting money opposite the Chanukah menorah] and the disdain [shown by covering the blood with one's foot].

According to the Ramban, the text of "Haneiros Halalu" states quite rightly that "these candles are holy" at the moment of the performance of the mitzvah—and that we are permitted to look at the Chanukah menorah, just as one was permitted to look at the menorah in the Beis Hamikdash, which was holy and whose oil was holy.

We are permitted to look at the Chanukah menorah

Just as it was forbidden to make use of the menorah in the Beis Hamikdash, so is it forbidden to make use of the Chanukah menorah (which the Sages consider comparable to *hekdesh*) at the time of the performance of the mitzvah. And just as it was permitted to look at the menorah in the Beis Hamikdash, whose light was truly holy, so is it permitted to look at the Chanukah menorah. For, as the Sages said, its light was meant to show all humanity that the Divine Presence rests upon Israel, for which reason, the menorah was outside the *paroches*. Indeed, in the Beis Hamikdash built by Shlomo Hamelech, the windows were designed to spread the light outward, and everyone could see it. Similarly, the Chanukah lights are meant to be seen and looked at. And this is all in addition to the halachic requirement of publicizing the miracle "in order to thank and to praise Your great name for Your miracles and for Your wonders and for Your salvation."

More allusions on tractate *Shabbos* 22

Rav Yosef is quoted in *Shabbos* 22—that reflects the story of the biblical Yosef and the twenty-two years that passed until the realization of his dreams—the narrative that we read in the weekly *parashah* that coincides with Chanukah.

Like the biblical Yosef, Rav Yosef waited twenty-two years until he became a "ruler"

The Gemara states:

> Rabbi Avin Halevi said: Whoever forces the moment, the moment forces him [back], but whoever yields to the moment, the moment yields itself to him.
>
> [This may be derived from an incident involving] Rabbah and Rav Yosef. Rav Yosef was [comparable to] "Sinai"—[i.e., his erudition was extraordinary]. And Rabbah [was] "one who uproots mountains"—[i.e., his brilliance was extraordinary]. A time came when they were needed, [and one would be chosen as head of the yeshiva].
> [The Sages of Bavel] sent [the following question to the Sages of the land of Israel]: What [sort of scholar] takes

precedence, a "Sinai" or "one who uproots mountains"?

[The Sages of Israel] replied to them: A "Sinai" takes precedence, because everyone needs [such a person, who is also referred to as] "the owner of the wheat," [i.e., he has encyclopedic knowledge of the source material].

Nevertheless, Rabbi Yosef did not accept [the position], because Chaldean [astrologers] had told him: "You will be [head of the yeshiva] for [only] two years."

Rabbah presided [as head of the yeshiva] for twenty-two years. [He then died, following which] Rav Yosef presided for two-and-a-half years.
During all those years that Rabbah presided, [Rav Yosef] did not even summon a [medical] bloodletter to his home—[i.e., he didn't assume even the slightest air of authority].

Berachos 64a

Rav Yosef waited twenty-two years until he reached his goal of standing at the head of the yeshiva, analogous to the twenty-two years Yosef waited until the realization of his destiny as ruler.

Rav Yosef was only able to solve a difficult question after the passage of twenty-two years

Rashi (ibid.) states that Rabbah was brilliant and was therefore called an "uprooter of mountains," whereas Rav Yosef was a master of halachah, mishnah and baraisa, and was therefore called "Sinai.

[The Sages] related:

> A certain matter was too difficult for Rabbah and Rav Yosef for twenty-two years and remained unresolved until Rav Yosef sat at the head [of the yeshiva] and solved it.
>
> *Kesubos* 42b

Rashi states that the twenty-years in which the matter remained unresolved were the years that Rabbah headed the yeshiva. When Rav Yosef subsequently became the head, heaven helped him solve this question so that he would attain a good reputation and stature. Rav Yosef, who had been known as "Sinai," was now helped by heaven after twenty-two years to "uproot mountains."

Correspondingly, we may say that this episode of Rav Yosef in Tractate *Shabbos* 22 alludes to the twenty-two years that passed until the dreams of Yosef's were actualized.

Rav Yosef possessed the qualities of "Sinai" and "uprooter of mountains"

After twenty-two years, Rav Yosef was able to solve a problem using the analytical skills possessed by an "uprooter of mountains." Indeed, we see in *Shabbos* 22 how Rav Yosef employed both deep analytical skill ("uprooter of mountains") and thoroughgoing knowledge ("Sinai") in comparing the law of the Chanukah candle to the law of covering the blood. Rav Yosef received help from heaven to engage in the analytics of Torah study in order to address the topic of treating a mitzvah with disdain "ביזוי מצוה", which is the central topic regarding the Chanukah light, and which is still the subject of in-depth and extensive discussion to this day.

Rav Yosef applied his innovative insight about treating a mitzvah with disdain to the matter of a Torah sage who forgot his learning

Rav Yosef, who taught that it is forbidden to treat a mitzvah with disdain, taught that the same is true of an older person who has forgotten his learning—i.e., it is forbidden to neglect his honor.

According to Rav Yosef, the Ark in the Mishkan contained both the second tablets and the fragments of the first tablets. The fragments of the first tablets allude to an older sage who has forgotten his learning. Just as the fragments were given the same honor as the complete set of tablets, so must we treat a sage who forgot his learning the same way we treat a sage who possesses his learning—i.e., with respect, and certainly not with disdain. (See *Bava Basra* 14b and *Berachos* 8b).

It is most apt that it was Rav Yosef who taught this, because—as we see in many places in the Talmud—he himself forgot his learning when he grew old and fell ill, yet we continue to relate to him with respect, as we do to anything that is holy or used in the performance of a mitzvah.

Let us conclude with the words of the Rambam:

The mitzvah of the Chanukah candle is very dear and beloved. A person must be careful with it in order to publicize the miracle and to enhance our praise of Hashem and our thanksgiving for the miracles He performed for us.

Hilchos Megillah Vechanukah 4:12

Parashas Vayigash

- **Upon meeting Yosef, Yaakov recited the *Sh'ma***
- **The reason that Yaakov recited the *Sh'ma* in particular**
- **Yaakov was unsure whether to believe his children**
- **Hashem appeared to Yaakov in a vision of the night because he had not yet regained the level of prophecy**
- **Hashem reassured Yaakov regarding two doubts that he harbored**
- **The fact that Yosef was fit to attend to Yaakov's burial shows that Yosef retained his state of holiness**

- **"And [Yosef] appeared to [Yaakov]" not only on the surface but also in an inner sense**
- **Targum Onkelos implies that Yaakov regained his prophetic ability**
- **Yaakov would reach such a level of holiness that Yosef would not be able to look at his face**

Why did Yaakov recite the *Sh'ma* when he saw Yosef after their twenty-two years of separation?

The Torah states:

כט. וירא אליו ויפל על צואריו ויבך על צואריו עוד:
בראשית מו:כט

29. And Yosef appeared to [Yaakov], and [Yosef] fell upon [Yaakov's] neck, and [Yosef] wept upon his neck for a long time.
Bereishis 46:29

Rashi comments:

> But Yaakov did not fall upon Yosef's neck, and he did not kiss him. Our Sages said, [this is because] he was reciting the *Sh'ma*.

Many great sages have strived to understand these extraordinary words of Rashi. Why did Yaakov choose to recite the *Sh'ma* specifically at the very moment that he met his beloved, precious son to whom his own soul was bound? Was this the time to recite the *Sh'ma*? Couldn't he have first hugged and kissed him and relieved his heart's infinite yearnings, and afterwards recited the *Sh'ma?*

The Ramban interprets this verse differently, based in part on the fact that "and he appeared to him" is superfluous. The Ramban says that it was the other way around; that it was Yaakov who cried on Yosef's neck.

But how may Rashi's words be understood?

Twenty-two years earlier, after Yosef was sold, his brothers brought his striped, blood-soaked coat to Yaakov, following which "he refused to be consoled" despite his children's oft-repeated attempts to comfort him. Rashi explains that this was because there is a heavenly decree upon a person who dies that after a period of time he will be sufficiently forgotten by the mourners for their pain to subside. Since Yosef was alive, however, Yaakov could not forget him.

Yaakov was unsure whether to accept his sons' words

Yaakov was steeped in worry and anguish because of a number of doubts he harbored. Should he have believed his sons that Yosef had been torn apart and was dead? When he saw that he was unable to accept consolation, that was apparently a sign that Yosef was still alive. Nevertheless, even if

Yosef was alive, how could Yaakov know that Yosef's holiness hadn't been impaired, and he wasn't spiritually lost forever? Yaakov was consumed by doubt and anguish because of these questions and, consequently, Divine inspiration did not rest upon him for the next twenty-two years.

And then, when his granddaughter Serach and afterwards his sons, informed Yaakov that Yosef was still alive, "his heart weakened, because he did not believe them" (*Bereishis* 45:26). Yaakov felt bad that he couldn't believe his sons when they reported Yosef's words to him. Only when he saw the carriages that Yosef sent "was his spirit revived"—i.e., Divine inspiration rested upon him again. What changed when Yaakov saw the carriages? Physically seeing the carriages, beyond relying upon his sons' testimony, verified for Yaakov that Yosef was indeed alive.

Yaakov's second concern was that perhaps Yosef hadn't maintained the supernal state of holiness fitting for him. But after Yaakov saw the carriages, when his sons testified that "Yosef is still alive" (ibid.), he understood—as the midrash states—that although Yosef was in a debauched land, he was still "alive" both spiritually and physically.

It was then that "Yisrael said, 'It is enough; My son Yosef is still alive. I will go and see him before I die" (*Bereishis* 45:28). And Rashi explains: "I am filled with joy and gladness because Yosef my son is still alive."

The Holy One, blessed be He, appeared to Yaakov only at night, because he had not yet regained full prophecy

Yaakov had not yet returned to his full greatness as a prophet; Hashem therefore spoke to Him in a night vision.

ג. ...אַל תִּירָא מֵרְדָה מִצְרַיְמָה כִּי לְגוֹי גָּדוֹל אֲשִׂימְךָ שָׁם:
ד. אָנֹכִי אֵרֵד עִמְּךָ מִצְרַיְמָה וְאָנֹכִי אַעַלְךָ גַם עָלֹה וְיוֹסֵף יָשִׁית יָדוֹ עַל עֵינֶיךָ:
בראשית מו:ג-ד

3. ..."Do not fear going down to Egypt, because I will make you into a great nation there.
4. "I will descend with you to Egypt, and I will also bring you up, and Yosef shall place his hand on your eyes."
Bereishis 46:3-4

The midrash relates that the Holy One, blessed be He, told Yaakov that Yosef would attend to him after he died, closing his eyes after his soul left his body. But how is this a reason for Yaakov not to fear going down to Egypt? We also need to understand more fully the nature of Yaakov's fears.

Perhaps it could be suggested that Yaakov had two concerns: 1) he was still afraid that Yosef's descent to Egypt had prevented him from rising to his proper state of holiness; 2) he feared that he himself might be harmed by the impure and debauched atmosphere of Egypt. Hashem therefore told him, "Do not fear going down to Egypt"—regarding your holiness. "I will go down with you to Egypt"—you will always cling to me. "And I will also bring you up"—even after you die, you will cling to Me. And a sign for this is that you will be buried in Ma'aras Hamakhpeilah in the Holy Land. And regarding your worry that the impure, debauched atmosphere of the land of Egypt will harm you, "Yosef will place his hand on your eyes (*einekhah*)," as understood by the Rashbam that Yosef will attend to all of Yaakov's affairs (*inyanekhah*).

Hashem reassured Yaakov regarding his two concerns

The Seforno writes:

[Hashem told Yaakov:]

> You will not [even] need to open your eyes to attain what you desire, because Yosef will bring it to you without your supervision. And you will not need to involve yourself with Egyptians who are unfit to approach you.

The midrash's statement that Yosef would attend to Yaakov when he died and would close Yaakov's eyes after his soul left does not contradict the statements of the Rashbam and the Seforno. Rather, it adds to what they wrote: Yosef would attend to his father throughout his sojourn in Egypt, even after his death.

The fact that Yosef was fit to attend to Yaakov's burial teaches us that Yosef had attained great holiness

However, the midrash is also communicating something beyond this. The Sages teach that "righteous people are greater in their death than in their lifetime" (*Chullin* 7b). Indeed, righteous people are very strict about the spiritual level of those who will attend to their bodies after their death. Here Hashem informed Yaakov that Yosef had attained the peak of righteousness and holiness, that he would outlive Yaakov and serve as the intermediary between the brothers and Yaakov, and that he alone was worthy of attending to Yaakov after his passing.

With that, Yaakov was assured that he had nothing to fear regarding a diminution of his own spiritual level in Egypt, and, furthermore, that Yosef's holiness was as elevated now as it had been when he was still with Yaakov. And with that, Yaakov was consoled for the twenty-two years he suffered during Yosef's absence.

"And he appeared to him"— with a penetrating inner gaze

When Yaakov and Yosef met, the Torah states that "[Yosef] appeared to [Yaakov]"—not in the sense that Yaakov saw him physically, but that Yaakov gazed at his inner being to determine: Is this the same Yosef who left his home as a person sanctified to Hashem? As we find elsewhere, great Torah personalities can look at a person and see whether his deeds are holy or the opposite. That is the meaning of "he appeared to him." It is not speaking of the body, but of an inner contemplation of the soul: Is Yosef "alive" in terms of his holiness and righteousness? (And that answers the question raised by the Ramban that this phrase seems to be superfluous.)

This understanding is supported by Targum Onkelos. When the Torah writes, "he appeared" in the context of a person appearing to another person, Onkelos translates it as "*ve'iskhazi*." But when the Torah writes "He appeared" in the context of Hashem appearing to a prophet, Onkelos translates it as "*ve'isgali*." And here Onkelos translates "and he appeared" as "*ve'isgali*." (See also *Sefer Shaarei Aharon*.)

"Ve'isgali" **refers to full prophecy in a fully awake state and not merely in a dream**

One may also say that Onkelos's translation, "*ve'isgali*," teaches us that when Yosef met Yaakov, Hashem appeared to Yaakov in a fully awake state of prophecy (and not merely in a dream), in keeping with His promise, "I will descend with you to Egypt." Yaakov was thus filled with joy: not only had he found his son Yosef but the Divine Presence was revealed to him in a waking state, as a result of which he experienced the highest level of revealed closeness to the Divine Presence. As a result, Yaakov felt the need to recite the *Sh'ma* at that elevated moment.

When Yaakov saw his son Yosef before him, and he saw that Yosef was spiritually whole and unblemished, a heavenly spirit descended upon him. What can compare to the great and elevated state of a father when he sees his beloved and dear son remaining firm in the ways of his forefathers? Immediately, Yaakov recited the *Sh'ma,* because now, after so many years, the Divine Presence was revealed to him, and he needed to greet and acknowledge his Creator with the highest declaration of faith and holiness.

Hashem hinted to Yaakov that he would attain such supernal holiness that Yosef would not be able to look upon him

When Yosef met his father, he saw the great holiness that rested upon him. Yaakov was on the level of the Kohen Gadol during the Kohen Gadol's blessing of the people. When the Kohanim bestow blessing upon the people, they are at that moment so holy it is forbidden to gaze upon them. Yosef thus placed his hand upon his father's eyes so that he would not gaze upon his father's extraordinary holiness.

And that is what Hashem had indicated to Yaakov in his dream: "Do not fear going down to Egypt; Yosef will place his hand upon your eyes"—meaning, as soon as you come to Egypt, you will attain such holiness that Yosef will need to place his hand over your eyes so as not to look into them. I would suggest that this may be where our universal and ancient custom to cover our eyes when we say the first verse of the *Sh'ma* has originated from.

Parashas Vayechi

I

- **"As for me, when I came from Padan"—why it is customary to teach this verse to schoolchildren**
- **Yaakov hinted to Yosef that he (Yosef) would be the next leader**
- **Yaakov indicated that he now understood everything Hashem had accomplished with the sale of Yosef**
- **The bond between Yaakov and Rachel, the mother of all Israel, produced Yosef, the leader of Israel**
- **In the merit of Rachel's generosity, the people of Israel will be strong until the end of all generations**
- **In order to inculcate this understanding in schoolchildren, we teach them this verse in particular**

II

- **Why the children of Israel are blessed specifically to be "like Ephraim and like Menashe"**
- **It is precisely Ephraim and Menashe who were in Egypt and remained holy who are fit to be the source of the blessing of children**
- **The reason the Levites were exempt from servitude in Egypt**
- **Yaakov could bestow a triple blessing**
- **Another reason that Rachel is the mother of all Israel**

III

- **Yosef wept because his brothers continued to think him capable of avenging himself against them**
- **The concluding theme of the Book of *Bereishis* is "unity"**
- **The unity of Israel comes from our faith that Hashem is one and His name is one**

I

"As for me, when I came from Padan"—why this verse is taught to schoolchildren with a special tune

a) The Torah states:

כט. ויקרבו ימי ישראל למות ויקרא לבנו ליוסף ויאמר לו אם נא מצאתי חן בעינך...

ה. ...אפרים ומנשה כראובן וכשמעון יהיו לי....

ז. ואני בבאי מפדן מתה עלי רחל....

29. When the time drew near for Israel to die, he called to his son Yosef, and he said to him, "If now I have found favor in your eyes....

5. "...Ephraim and Menashe shall be mine like Reuven and Shimon....

7. "As for me, when I came from Padan, Rachel died upon me...."

Bereishis 47:9, 48:5,7

Why did Yaakov now tell Yosef about his mother Rachel? "As for me, when I came from Padan, Rachel died upon me in the land of Canaan on the way, when there was still a stretch of land to come to Efrat. And I buried her there on the way to Efrat, which is Beis Lechem" (*Bereishis* 48:7). Also requiring explanation is why this verse, accompanied by Rashi's commentary, is taught to schoolchildren with a special tune.

After Yaakov told Yosef about Rachel, Yaakov saw Yosef's children, Ephraim and Menashe, and he blessed them with the eternal blessing that every Jewish parent blesses his children, "May G-d make you like Ephraim and like Menashe."

There are three surprising elements here:

1. Why is this, more than any other statement of Yaakov's, taught to schoolchildren?
2. Why did Yaakov choose this moment to tell this to Yosef, and not earlier?
3. What does "I buried her there on the way to Efrat, which is Beis Lechem," teach us?

Rashi quotes the midrash that Yaakov buried Rachel there so that when her children go into exile, they pass by her grave and she will pray on their behalf as she weeps— "Rachel weeps for her children" (*Yirmiyahu* 31:14)—and in her merit, "the children will return to their border."

Yosef perpetuated Yaakov's leadership

Perhaps Yaakov's intent was to hint to Yosef that now, at the conclusion of Yaakov's life, Yosef's final mission was the work of uniting all the people of Israel, and of being the leader and emblem for all generations. We might further say that on that occasion the obligation to continue the leadership of the nation of Israel was placed upon Yosef. Therefore, Yosef was obligated to unite all of the brothers and heal the discord among them.

Furthermore, Yaakov hinted to Yosef that from now on his mother Rachel would be the primary mother of all the tribes. She had merited this due to her nobility, kindness, and supreme self-sacrifice, which she exhibited when she surrendered her own happiness for the sake of her sister, Leah, helping her get married to Yaakov despite knowing that Yaakov had served Lavan for seven years in order to marry *her,* Rachel. Rachel had performed this noble deed so that Leah would not be shamed. Rachel's act thus surpassed even the lofty mitzvah of "You shall love your neighbor as yourself," because she went beyond mere love and sacrificed her own happiness for the sake of her sister. For this, she earned the merit of being the mother of the nation of Israel.

Yaakov felt responsible for Rachel's death

Therefore, it was specifically at this point, after so many years of being separated and nearing the end of his life, that Yaakov told Yosef that he now felt consoled for Rachel's death, and he now understood the entire chain of events. Yaakov told Yosef, "When I came from Padan, Rachel died upon me." מתה עלי רחל What does "upon me" mean? Yaakov had used the same phrase earlier: "And I will bring a curse *upon me*"והבאתי עלי קללה (*Bereishis* 27:12) . Here too, it may be suggested that "upon me" alludes to a curse: Yaakov had cursed whoever had stolen Lavan's *teraphim,* not knowing that Rachel had done so. As a result, Yaakov felt that he himself had unintentionally brought about Rachel's death, as a *tzadik's* curse always comes true.

"And that," Yaakov told Yosef, "resulted in all the days of the pain suffered by me, by your mother, and by you, when you went missing from me. And when I saw that I could not attain consolation, I understood that you must still be alive. And then I prayed on your behalf, referring to you as 'Yosef son of Rachel,' since she too cries for her children. And then I recalled all of the troubles that I had undergone."

In the merit of Rachel, the people of Israel will exist until the end of all generations

"And now," Yaakov told Yosef, "I have come to learn that everything Hashem did was for the good. He withheld His anger and did not take the life of your mother, Rachel, immediately, even though it is possible for the curse of a sage to be actualized immediately." (The Talmud records instances in which a sage gazed upon someone and immediately "turned him into a heap of bones.") "When Rachel came to the border of the land of Israel, she was able to complete the nation by giving birth to Binyamin, the 12th tribe. She passed away in a spot where her sons could prostrate themselves at her grave, and she would hasten their redemption. She merited this because she surrendered her marriage to Yaakov that night for the sake of her sister. The Holy One, blessed be He, rewarded her for this by extending the days of her life with kindness and compassion."

We learn from this episode that the foundation and basis of the life of every Jewish man and woman is Rachel's kindness and her weeping for her children. Thus, in the parents' blessing for daughters ישמך א-להים כשרה רבקה רחל ולאה, Rachel is mentioned before Leah, because the house of Israel exists in the merit of Rachel's acts of kindness. Indeed, as Rashi states, "even the children of Leah acknowledge that Rachel is the mainstay of the house" (see Rashi to *Rus* 4:11). And so, this is why schoolchildren are taught the phrase 'When I came from Padan...' with particular emphasis. The intention is to instill in them the idea that the house of Israel, the nation of kindness, was built through the power of Rachel's generosity and forbearance.

II

The reason we bless our children to be specifically "like Ephraim and Menashe"

"May G-d make you like Ephraim and Menashe" ישמך א-להים כאפרים וכמנשה (*Bereishis* 48:20).

Why do we bless our children to be specifically like Ephraim and Menashe, and not like the other tribes? A deep meaning is embedded here: although Ephraim and Menashe were born in a land of debauched impurity, they were elevated in Torah and holiness. So too the people of Israel, who will pass through all the exiles in the impure lands of the nations, are blessed that they too, like Ephraim and Menashe, rise in Torah and the fear of heaven despite all the vicissitudes and storms of the days of exile. This is why the custom of the holy people of Israel to recite this blessing every Shabbos, as Shabbos is the source of blessing, including the blessing for the weekdays (which correspond to the exile).

To grow in holiness and Torah even in a debauched land

"Hear, my son, the teaching of your father" (*Mishlei* 1:8).

Yaakov told Yosef: "I did not imagine that the people of Israel could maintain their righteousness in an elevated way in the impurity of the land of Egypt. But I saw that all that Hashem did, He did for His own sake. You were in Egypt for so many years, yet you are nevertheless the leader of Israel, and from your very own children we see that the Jewish people can hold firm even in the storms of the exile. Your children will be a paradigm for the people of Israel at all times, on the level of 'the deeds of the fathers are a sign for the children,' since you are the leader of Israel in the exile."

We see that the great *rishonim*—Rambam, Ramban and Abarbanel—were royal advisors, ministers, and treasurers, and they illuminated the people of Israel in the exile. When Yaakov blessed Reuven, Shimon, and Levi, he emphasized their obligation to unite the nation so that the people would be like one person with one heart, as baseless hatred was the cause of the second Temple's destruction.

Shimon and Levi: from curse to blessing

My father wrote a wonderful essay, which for the Torah journal *Hapardes*, on why the tribe of Levi was exempt from servitude in Egypt.

In that essay, he raises the following question: Yaakov rebuked Shimon and Levi with the words, "Cursed is their anger because it is strong" (*Bereishis* 49:7), yet Moshe praised them (*Devarim* 48:7-8 and Rashi to 8). My father explained that Yaakov rebuked them for their harsh nature, which Levi took to heart, repented, and transformed his innate traits to goodness, and when he accomplished that and influenced his tribe, then Moshe Rabbeinu praised them.

Yaakov's triple blessing

The nation of Israel stands on three pillars: Avraham, Yitzchak, and Yaakov.

Yaakov told his sons: "Since I am the last of the forefathers, I have triple power to bless you. This is in addition to the power of blessing I received from having acquired the first-born status from Eisav, which made me a Kohen and thus empowered me to administer the blessing of a Kohen—"Birkas Kohanim" (*Bamidbar* 6:23-27)." And the midrash states that the blessing Yaakov received from the angel (Sar Shel Eisav)he wrestled with the entire night was "Birkas Kohanim," with which he now blessed his sons.

The character of a "stiff-necked people"

The Gemara tells:

Yaakov sought to reveal the end of days to his sons, but the Divine Presence left him. He said, "Perhaps, heaven forbid, there was something unfit in my fathering of these children...." His sons told him, "Hear O Israel, Hashem our G-d, Hashem is one. Just as in your heart there is only one, so too in our hearts there is only one."

Pesachim 56a

The survival of the Jewish people through the generations of exile is driven by our unbreakable stubborn faith. The people of Israel are "a stiff-necked people," but there are two sides to that, one negative, one positive. On the one hand, we have survived because of it, and on the other hand, we have survived despite it, steadfastly maintaining our belief with wonderous obstinacy. Our faith remains strong because of our love for Hashem and our love for each other, two mitzvos that come from the heart, mitzvos that we were taught by Yaakov (who himself combined two opposite qualities: kindness, which is warm and justice, which is cold).

We require these two qualities in order to survive in the exile until the end of days.

An additional reason why Rachel is the mother of all Israel

One can posit another reason why Rachel merited to be the mother of all Israel: Hashem extended her life until she gave birth to Binyamin, whose entry into the world made the tribes twelve in number. Together with Yaakov, they were thirteen in number, thirteen having the numerical value of "*echad,*" **אח"ד** "one." This idea is reflected in the verse, "Israel, one nation upon the land" גוי **אחד** בארץ (*Shmuel* 2 7:23).

Binyamin is the central, concluding link that unites us into one nation. This is why Binyamin's portion of the land of Israel includes Jerusalem and the Beis Hamikdash, for the Beis Hamikdash is the center of Israel and the place where all the tribes come on pilgrimage. This is reflected in the verse, "Jerusalem that is built like a city that is bound together" (*Tehillim* 122:3).

The Torah states:

יז. כה תאמרו ליוסף אנא שא נא פשע אחיך וחטאתם כי רעה גמלוך ועתה שא נא לפשע עבדי אלקי אביך ויבך יוסף בדברם אליו:

בראשית נ:יז

17. "So shall you say to Yosef: Please forgive your brothers' sin and their transgression, because they did evil to you. And now please forgive the sin of the servants of the G-d of your father." And Yosef wept when they spoke to him.

Bereishis 50:17

Rashi comments:

They altered the facts for the sake of peace, as Yaakov had not given such a command, as he did not suspect Yosef [of this].

Yosef wept because his brothers suspected him unjustly after he had treated them kindly for so many years, not only refraining from taking revenge against them also ensuring that they received the choicest territory in Egypt.

III

Why Yosef wept before his brothers

Previously, when Yosef had cried, he had "turned aside from [his brothers] and wept" (*Bereishis* 42:4). This time, however, he didn't do so: Rather, "Yosef wept when they spoke to him."

It appears that in this instance Yosef chose to weep before his brothers in order to demonstrate the pain he felt from the fact that they didn't trust him to treat them with justice, kindness, and compassion but suspected him of wishing to avenge himself against them and harm them. Perhaps at that moment Yosef rose to the level of the Kohen Gadol, who weeps when he is suspected by the elders of the court (see m. *Yoma* 1:5).

Sefer Bereishis concludes with the theme of unity

Parashas Vayechi is the last *parashah* of the Book of *Bereishis,* and "the last is the most beloved" אחרון אחרון חביב (*Bereishis Rabbah*). The final theme of the book is the completion of the circuit upon which the existence of unity depends. And in the merit of this unity, the Divine Presence, which is the soul of the united nation, rests upon us.

The siddur states, "You are one and Your name is one and who is like Your nation Israel, one nation in the land." And the *Zohar* states, "Israel, the Torah, and the Holy One, blessed be He, are one" (*Zohar* 3:73).

It is interesting that the theme of unity also corresponds to the end of the book of *Shemos*. Moshe Rabbeinu was upset that he had not participated in the building of the Mishkan. But the Holy One, blessed be He, had kept the most beloved work for him, to be performed last: the erecting of the Mishkan. "So shall the Mishkan become one" (*Shemos* 26:6).

The conclusion of the Mishkan brings about unity and causes the Divine Presence to rest upon us. And so "the last is most beloved."

Let us conclude with a blessing that may be realized in us always: "Bless us, our Father, all of us as one, in the light of Your countenance" (siddur).

ברכנו אבינו כלנו כאחד באור פניך

In Conclusion and in Celebration

There are many Torah sources regarding the importance of birthdays and commemorating them. The Gemara speaks expressly about the importance of celebrating one's sixtieth birthday:

"When Rabbi Yosef was sixty years old, he made a celebration for the Rabbis He said, "I have outlived the period in which a person may die from *kareis*" (*Moed Katan* 28a).

I merited to conduct myself accordingly when I turned sixty, in keeping with the advice of my teacher, Rabbi Dovid Cohen שליט"א.

When my seventieth birthday was drawing near, I thought, "How much more so I am obligated to celebrate this great milestone in life, and I should buy something new so that I will be able to recite the blessing of ***shehecheyanu***", to praise Hashem for giving me life. To that end, I bought myself a new tallis.

To know specifically when I should recite the blessing of ***shehecheyanu*** on the tallis and for guidance how to properly observe the event of my 70th birthday, I again turned to Rabbi Cohen. He referred me to Responsa *Chavos Yair* **70**, which addresses the importance of a person's **seventieth** birthday and discusses the blessing of ***shehecheyanu*** **for the birthday itself** (without the need for a new garment or fruit!), and whether the celebration in its honor is a *seudas mitzvah,* and related issues. That responsum was printed in its entirety in the Hebrew edition of this book. I felt it would benefit the readers as there the *Chavos Yair* discusses **all the festivities of the entire life cycle**! I broke up the text into paragraphs and bolded the beginning of every entry so the reader can easily find the laws of celebration of whichever life event he wants to look up. The responsum is included in the Hebrew edition, in this volume, I will delight the reader with a brief biographical sketch of the *Chavos Yair*.

After a little research, I learned that many rabbis have discussed this responsum and expanded on the topic. Like everything in the holy Torah, there are various views and outlooks. For the present, however, we will only point out that in his later years on his birthday the ***Chafetz Chaim*** would recite the blessing of ***Shehecheyanu*** (some say that he would have something new as well, to further bolster the need to say ***Shehecheyanu***) and make a modest celebration to which he invited his greatest students, Rabbi Elchanan Wasserman זצ"ל and Rabbi Yosef Shlomo Kahaneman זצ"ל, the Rosh yeshiva of Ponevezh. This topic is extensive and calls for its own essay. For the present, with the conclusion of the first volume of *Chamudei Shai*, I only want to express my personal thoughts and feelings regarding this milestone in my life.

The verse states, "The days of our years are **seventy years**, and with might, eighty years" (*Tehillim* 90:10). It appears to me that the simple meaning of this verse is that these seventy years constitute an entire life. After 70 years, every additional year and even every new day is a new life, a gift from the Hashem. (I heard about a great Sephardic rabbi from a few generations ago who did not celebrate his birthday until he reached the age of seventy, and from then on, he celebrated every year, because each year is the gift of a new life from Hashem.)

The letter **ע** ***ayin*** has the numerical value of seventy, and the word ***ayin*** means "eye," the most important sensory organ, which sees and perceives the world. When a person reaches the age of seventy, we may say that he receives new vision, lenses of a new prescription that have been crafted by his seventy years of experience. At this age, we attain a **עין טובה** - ***ayin tova,*** a good eye, one that focuses on the good in the world.

I figure that if my life is renewed every day, then I have newly updated vision daily, and I can keep more fully the prescription, "**Every day** [the words of the Torah] **should be new in your eyes**" (Rashi on *Shemos* 19:1): to see everything anew every day—"**New every morning**, vast is Your faithfulness" (*Eichah* 3:23)—with the vision of a "**good eye**" of the seventy years of wisdom attained by the experience of a full life.

All these feelings may be encapsulated in the verse, ארך ימים אשביעהו ואראהו בישועתי "I will satiate him with length of days, and I will show him My salvation" (*Tehillim* 91:16). When we recite this verse in prayer, we recite it twice. What does that custom mean?

The first time we say this verse, it is both in the national and the individual sense. In the national sense, Hashem gives the Jewish people a long history **satiated with all good** and that is in the **present**, and in the **future** "I will **show him My salvation**" via the sovereign Moshiach and the attainment of all the aspirations of the future. In the individual sense, "I will **satiate** him with **length of days**" means that **a person's life is filled with all good every day**; and moreover, "I will show him

My **salvation**" means that **Hashem saves each individual from all of his troubles**.

As for the repetition of the verse, perhaps that is in keeping with the verse, "I am my beloved's and my beloved's is mine" (*Shir Hashirim* 6:3). Our relationship with Hashem must be "**face-to-face**", reciprocal. We must give Him like He gives us, not only as a sign of gratitude but also so that He will continue to give. To merit the physical **length of days**, we must "**satiate**" i.e. fill every moment of our "length of days" with Torah study, prayer and good deeds, as we pray every day in the evening prayer: "...for **they** (the words of Torah) **are our lives** and **lengthen our days** and in them (the words of Torah) we will **engage day and night".** When we do so, we **"satiate Hashem",** as it were. Therefore, "**I** [the human being] will satiate **Him** [Hashem] with **length of days**" - a Jew's "**length of days**" is not just "full", but **"satiating to Hashem**", with his Torah study, prayer, and good deeds[7].

But we must add to that, "I will **show Him - <u>my</u> salvation**" – the fact that I am saved by Hashem. We must show Hashem, and the whole world, our

---

[7] That is the central point of the second section of *Nefesh Hachaim*: that our service of Hashem is called His **"sustenance"** — that because of our providing Hashem with our Torah and the mitzvos, and with our prayer in particular, He will dwell within us, just as when we eat physical food our soul will dwell in our body.

recognition and appreciation with our song and praise for how Hashem always saves us constantly.

I related this this thought more than a decade ago to my teacher, Rabbi Shmuel Kamenetsky שליט"א, rosh yeshiva of Philadelphia, and it found favor in his eyes and he voiced his approval.

"Rabbi Elazar ben Azaria said: I am like [but not quite] seventy years old".
(*Berachos* 1:5)

Not long ago, I was not quite seventy,
now I have surpassed seventy,
blessed be G-d of eternity,
that I have reached sagacity

Blessed be Hashem for eternity, amen and amen.
ב'רוך י' ל'עולם א'מן ואמן

A Brief Biographical Sketch of the Chavos Yair

Rabbi Yair Chayim Bachrach, known by his work "**Chavos Yair**" was a major Jewish scholar in the 17th century. Besides his outstanding expertise in Halacha (Jewish law), which is the mainstay of the "Chavos Yair" and his other books, he had complete mastery of all areas of Torah including Kabbalah, and he was well versed in the sciences, music, history and wrote poetry.

He was born either in 1638 or 1639. His original name was Chaim, the name Yair ("To Shine" – future tense) was added because an illness as a way of getting mercy from Heaven to recover "and continue to shine". Generally, in such cases the name "Chaim" (life) is added, but as that was his name already, this wasn't applicable.

He tells his life story in his books (we have only 2%); his later books pick up where he left off in his earlier books. He does not write about his childhood or adolescence. It is amazing how he tells his life story in full detail and it's all in poetic style and rhymes! In what was supposed to be his Magnum opus, the "*Eitz HaChaim*" (more on this unpublished book later), he says that when he was 23 he received the highly distinguished ordination, called "*Moreinu*", a title previously never awarded to a Torah scholar under 40 years of age..

When he was just 24, he lectured at the "*Yerid*", the grand commerce and trade fair in Frankfurt. The Grand Fair was for the purpose of doing commerce, but it was an opportunity for great rabbis from across the world to meet each other. Many decisions of **ועד ארבע ארצות - Council of Four Lands** were taken and signed at the "*Yerid*". At this great "convention", he lectured all the rabbis in attendance (which included the greatest of world Jewry), and his lectures "found favor in their eyes and were well received". He writes that during this period of his life "he was beloved by all the congregations in Germany". At the age of 28, he was received as the Rav of the city of Koblenz and the environs, and there he was actually "very happy and prosperous", but it only lasted "3 years and a few days." At the end of that time, he was persecuted with great hatred. He wrote that he did not want to record the details of that affair because he did not want to bring shame on anyone. He accepted his lot and in the beginning of the winter of 1670 he moved to the town of Worms where his father was serving as rabbi. By the summer, his father, who had been the rabbi there for 20 years, passed away. His father left a passionate request in his will to the town of Worms to for his son to take over the rabbinate in his place.

But as is the way of politics, his father's dying wish was not honored. The community leaders gave the excuse that they had a policy of not taking "one of their own laymen" as their rabbi and he was a **בעל בית**. Asides from his outstanding greatness, he had not resided as a "layman" in Worms for even 6 months! Nonetheless, the community hired another rabbi, Rav Ahron Teomin - Frankel. The *Chavos Yair* continued to live in Worms and maintained a cordial relationship with the elected rabbi, and even though he wrote criticisms to some of the elected rabbi's books, he nonetheless took a "Haskama" (approbation) from the elected rabbi for his book "*Mekor Chaim*" (more on this book later).

He remained in Worms until the 13th of Sivan 1689 when the city was destroyed by the French in the Nine Years' War. The entire Jewish population went into exile, and many, including himself, sought refuge in Frankfurt. Frankfurt had a Jewish printing press, and he himself had published there years earlier (see below). Now being resident in Frankfurt, it gave him the drive to print some of the massive amount of material he had in manuscript form. We will now survey what we know he had, and what was ultimately brought to print.

The "Yair Netiv"

Rav Bachrach was a genius in all areas of Torah and secular knowledge (even in the art of poetry), and he had extensive writings on all these topics. By his own estimation, what he ultimately printed was only 1/50th of what he had in writing. His writings were so voluminous that he had to write a directory to keep track of them. The directory catalogues every topic he wrote on and was called "Yair Netiv" (which includes his name "Yair") which means "lighting the path. It is a whole book in its own right! It was never published, but remains in manuscript and can be viewed online

"Eitz HaChaim"

He was working on an encyclopedic work called "*Eitz HaChaim*" (which includes his name "Chaim") and it would have nine major disciplines corresponding to the nine letters of the the words **חסד פחד אמת** (kindness, fear, truth). The disciplines included Faith, Mitzvos, Discourses, Talmud, Anecdotes, Original ideas of Torah ("Chidushei Torah"), Proper conduct ("Derech Eretz"), Piety ("Chassidus"), and Sermons. He felt that his huge amount of material, "the equivalent of several books", wasn't properly edited and he didn't have the strength or the funds to properly prepare such a massive project for print. He promised that some of the material would be featured in his "smaller books" on the Shulchan Aruch, of which he only completed the section on "Orach Chaim". We will discuss that work below. **"Mar Kashisha"**

This book was probably originally part of the "Eitz HaChaim". It explains Talmudic terms, expressions, "tendencies", and its logical constructs. It also explains the guidelines to make Halachic rulings. It was not brought to the press in his lifetime, and was only published from manuscript centuries later by Machon Yerushalayim **"Mekor Chaim"**.

Then there is the sad story of the "Mekor Chaim", which was going to be a book on the Orach Chaim section of the Shulchan Aruch. He researched and revealed the sources) for all the rulings of the "Mechaber" (Rabbi Yosef Karo) and the "Rema" (Rabbi Moshe Isserles). In addition to that, he recorded new rulings that were formulated over the course of previous generations, and his own rulings and customs. This book was ready to be published by 1679. Prior to publishing, copies were sent to the great Rabbis of the generation (including the elected Rabbi in Worms, as we wrote above) and he received very enthusiastic approbations. However, out of respect for his father and grandfather, who were already deceased, he delayed publishing his own book to put out a book of their responsa, which he called "Chut HaShani" (Scarlet ribbon). The "Chut HaShani" was published in Frankfurt in 1679, and the printing of the "Mekor Chaim" was delayed for years.

Before he got a chance to print the "Mekor Chaim" the "Meginei Eretz" (Shields of the Earth), which was an edition of the Orach Chaim section of the Shulchan Aruch with the commentaries of the "Magen Avraham" (by Rabbi Avraham Gombiner) and the "Magen David" (by Rabbi David Segal - AKA the **TAZ**) was released. To his surprise, he found that they had already done most of the research that he did, which he writes about in several places. In one place (Chavos Yair siman 9), he writes that 2/3 of the "Mekor Chaim" was already in the "Meginei Eratz". He further states that in some cases where they ruled differently than he did, he actually felt that they were right! However, he also saw some of their rulings that he disagreed with, as well as certain "imperfections" that he took issue with. **But either way, he had to revise his book radically before bringing it to press**. This massive revision was not finalized in his lifetime, and the book was notprinted, until parts of it were found in 1982 and printed by Machon Yerushalayim.

"Chavos Yair"

During his 10 years in Frankfurt, he was determined to finally bring to press whatever he deemed ready for publication. This resulted in collation and publication of his responsa by which he is known for posterity as the "**Chavos Yair**", published in 1699.

In these responsa, he had an interesting style of only mentioning the name of the one making the inquiry if he was already deceased, but he would not name the inquirer if he was still alive.

He explains himself in his introduction:

"*.......the answer for this* (only naming the deceased and not the living) *is clear and something that is self-evidently true that since [the inquirer is] a great man that both likes me and is also sparring with me is still alive, May Hashem lengthen his days, I did not want to make him public by name lest he may not want that, on the one hand that people will say that a "lion" (expression for greatness) like him is now a (שואל* inquirer) *to a (שועל* fox - expression for lowliness) *like me. And even though often I also asked him (the* *inquirer) questions, he is worthy to be asked and not an inquirer. Also, sometimes "my son did not go down with him"* (poetic way of saying "I did not agree with him")*, rather I criticize his opinion based on a Gemara or from logic and I clarified that he overlooked something or is in error, most people would surely be upset with this, and it would seem as if "I have a shining face" (happy/ taking pride) that I have argued on him and I've had Joy in his failure, G-d forbid [for me to take honor in that]......... Therefore, I said to hide [his name] is what is necessary and praiseworthy. This is not the case regarding the Geonim of earlier generations, the pillars of the world, the greats of the generation that already went to the life of the world to come and are in the world of truth. They surely would be pleased with their names mentioned because over there is no jealousy, no haughtiness, and no trickery".*

His Humility

He goes on to write that if anyone attacks his opinions, he will not take any offense whatsoever. If someone would refute any of his positions with ample proof from Torah sources or straight thinking, he would only be grateful for the truth coming out. If in the heat of an argument someone would call him "not even [as learned as] a shepherd of sheep" he would just answer: "I am even less. I am not even [as learned as] the assistant of a shepherd of sheep!". However, he qualifics this stoic attitude only for those that genuinely want to battle him in a legitimate battle of Torah ideas. But anyone who just attacks him for no reason whatsoever, on this there is no forgiveness, not for the sake of his own honor as he doesn't possess even "an eighth of an eighth" of pride (but rather for the pure evil of the opponent attacking his Torah for no reason). He disregards all the titles and lavish praise heaped on him by the Rabbis writing to him, and he erased all the titles and praise in the letters, although sometimes he missed the opportunity to erase the title or praise (or the copyist or printer put the praises back in the book, even though they were crossed out).

The Name "Chavos Yair"

There is great significance to the name "Chavos Yair" that attests to his humility and deep poetic soul, as he writes in his introduction to his sefer:

*"And since the new rulings that have emerged are light and without depth and sharpness of the "Battle of Torah" and not of great artistry, I called the name of the responsa "**Chavos Yair**" because they are to me, relative to the responsa of the great ones, like scattered villages*

that have no wall (which were the biblical Chavos Yair), *relative to fortified walled cities that are fortified up to the heavens. Furthermore, my name that was given to me by heaven when I was ill, is Yair, and "Chavos" can also mean life, like the meaning of the name* **"Chava"** *in the simple meaning of the word, which alludes to the name given to me after birth Chaim* (life). *Another reason for this name* (Chavos Yair) *is an allusion, as I realized the number of responsa standing fully ready for print are at least 635 – gematria* (numerical value) *חות* יאיר (Chavos Yair)".

But that's not all…

His Grandmother Chava Bachrach – an Exceptional Woman

"*Aside from all this, I also chose this name to be a good remembrance for my pious grandmother Chava zt"l, the mother of my father, the Gaon Rabbi Shimshon, for she is worthy of this, whether because of her I have the lineage on my father's side to the "Crown of Glory", the well-known Gaon who is mentioned by all the authors Rabbi Leib of Prague* (the **Maharal** of Prague)*……as my grandmother was the daughter of his* (the Maharal's) *daughter, the wife of Rabbi Yizchak Cohen, who was called by all "Reb Itzik* (Yitzchak) *Reb Leib's" as a tribute to his father-in-law, the Gaon Rabbi Leib of*

Prague..... She is also deserving of this because of her erudition. She was one of a kind in her generation in Torah. *I know that she had a Midrash Rabbah without any commentaries and she learned it relying on her understanding and intelligence -- and in many instances, she argued on the rabbi, the author of "Matnos Kehuna"* (a leading commentary on the Midrash Rabbah) *and explained the Midrash differently, and anyone [really] listening could discern that she was right! I wrote some of her ideas in my books in her name. She was accomplished in the commentaries on the Machzorim, in the commentary of Rashi on Chumash and the 24 books of Tanach,* **in the** *Targumim* (Aramaic translations of Tanach), *and the "external books"* (books of wisdom not part of Tanach or the oral law). *There were several times that the great ones of the generation were confused about a topic, and she came and offered them the answer. She was outstanding in her writing with a very clear polished language.*

She was also outstanding in her piousness and ethical conduct in a manner that's impossible to describe on paper. She was widowed when she was only 30 years old and never married again in honor of her husband, my grandfather, the Gaon Rabbi Shmuel. I heard from the holy mouth of my master, my father the Gaon Rabbi Shimshon, that the Gaon and Chossid [saint] Rabbi Yeshayahu [Horowitz] z"tl, the author of the Shnei Luchos [HaBris] (known as the Shelah HaKadosh), *when he emigrated from the diaspora to the land of Israel, he wanted to marry her, but she was not willing. He* (the Shelah HaKadosh) *said: "my sins caused that I did not merit to connect to such a holy entity!"*

She lived in Prague, the home of her ancestors, and when "the ark of Hashem embarked", and my master, my father, the Gaon zt"l left Prague in the year 1650 where he served as preacher, to the holy congregation of Worms to serve as rabbi, she came with him. She was with him for about a year, and after that she embarked on a journey to the land of Israel. In our great sins, she did not make it, but rather died in the community of Sofia in the "land of Turkey" (Ottoman empire, today Sofia is capital of Bulgaria). *Thehonor that they gave her in her death was truly wondrous, and so also* (she was honored greatly) *in every place she ever visited because her name was well known. The 'scent' of her high level spread throughout all the countries, in addition to her lineage and the honor of her two great brothers, the great Geonim the rabbis of Poland, the Gaon Rabbi Chaim Katz the Av Beis Din of Posen, who previously had been the rabbi of Frankfurt It is impossible to exaggerate how much honor these two brothers who were geniuses gave to their sister, my grandmother.*

Because all my other ancestors were men of great fame and composed many books full of wisdom, their remembrance are their words, and they have sons who carry on the family name, let alone that they (the sons) *are also wise men and "the trunk attests to its roots". None of these [rememberances] are applicable to women so I therefore made my grandmother a remembrance because in her wisdom of Torah and good deeds she was the "mother of her generation" and a crown of glory. We can also understand the term Chavos Yair as Chava'sYair* (with ashkenazic pronunciation, in Yiddish) *i.e. Yair who belongs to Chava........."*

As written above, the "Teshuvos Chavos Yair" was only intended to be 1/50 of his writings, and even it is smaller than intended. As he wrote in the introduction, he intended to bring 635 responsa to press, and in the conclusion of the book, he acknowledges that he only brought 221 responsa to press, which is the numerical value of יאיר (Yair). He then added another 11 responsa, totaling 232, so it should have the numerical value of יהי אור (let there be light), and he ends off with a lengthy deep kabbalistic discourse on יהי אור (let there be light), which is further evidence of his great expertise in Kabbalah, even though he cautioned people from engaging in it, lest they misunderstand.

A Poet and Songwriter

The Chavos Yair was a poet, but what is amazing is that he could write whole paragraphs of academic substance, whether Torah ideas or history, and these long paragraphs would be rhythmical. He was also gifted with a musical sense and a fine singing voice. Rabbi Yuzpa Shamash of Worms wrote regarding him in his book "Minhagim of Worms":

"We could not find in our congregation [another] Chazzan like him, be it in the knowledge of the Machzor and its meanings with all the Kavanos (intentions)-- because he is very sharp and erudite, and a man of learning who is great and important --[be it] in Chazzanus [in general], and particularly the tunes of Chazzanus that pertain to the Yomim Noraim, for he is a great artist in the art of Chazzanus and has a pleasant voice."

Rabbi Yuzpa records that in the year 1671, even though the *Chavos Yair* was in the year of *aveilus* (mourning) for his father, nonetheless, the congregation implored him to be the Chazzan for Shacharis on the first day of Rosh HaShana and for Mussaf on Yom Kippur. They later asked him to be Chazzan for *Tefilas Geshem* on Shmini Atzeres, but he refused them because of his *aveilus* (mourning).

Chavos Yair Composed Last Stanza of Maoz Tzur

With his poetic soul and tendency towards song, he composed poems, including an additional stanza to the *Maoz Tzur* recited on Chanukah! This stanza would be in place of today's final stanza חשוף זרוע קדשך.... which had not yet been composed and added in his time.

The first version was:

חוֹקֵר לֵב וָקֶרֶב / רְאֵה נָא בְּעָנְיֵנוּ
יוֹצֵר בֹּקֶר וָעֶרֶב / הַבִּיטָה בְּשִׁפְלוּתֵנוּ
יְהִי קֵץ לְגָלוּתֵנוּ / בְּנֵה בֵּית מִקְדָּשֵׁנוּ

מַגֵּר אַדֶּרֶת / שֵׂעִיר הַגּוֹבֶרֶת
וְתִשְׁכֹּן בְּקִרְבֵּנוּ / מַהֵר וְהוֹאֵל
שְׁלַח הַגּוֹאֵל / מְשִׁיחַ צִדְקֵנוּ

Which translates (roughly) as:

He who sees into the heart and innards
see please our afflictions
He who fashioned morning and evening
look at our downtrodden state
let there be an end to our exile
build our Beis HaMikdash
destroy [he who is] the cloak of
hair (referring to Eisov-Edom) *who is [currently]*
dominating
and dwell in our midstquick!
And be willing

send the redeemer
Moshiach our righteous

This piece received criticism for two reasons:

1) The Maoz Tzur is written in singular form and this addition is in plural form and thus asymmetrical

2) He relied on ending words with נו (our) to make the rhyme scheme and that is "not so impressive"

He took the criticism to heart, but didn't get discouraged, and he revised the stanza as follows:

חוֹקֵר לֵב וָקֶרֶב / אָבִי מַלְכִּי וְקוֹנִי
יוֹצֵר בֹּקֶר וָעֶרֶב / רְאֵה נָא בְּעָנְיִי
יָדְךָ הָרֵם עַל מוֹנִי / הָרִאשׁוֹן אַדְמוֹנִי
מַגֵּר אַדֶּרֶת / שֵׂעִיר הַגּוֹבֶרֶת
נָחָשׁ הקדמוני / ואז יִגְדַּל שְׂשׂוֹנִי

Which translates (roughly) as:

He who sees into the heart and innards
my father my king my master
He who fashioned morning and evening

see please my affliction
your hand raise against my oppressor
the first[born] who is red
destroy [he who is] the cloak of
hair (referring to Eisav-Edom) *who is [currently] dominating*
the original snake (alluding to the Kabbalistic concept that the evil of Edom is rooted in the snake of Eden)
and then great will be my joy

Back to Worms

During his 10 years in Frankfurt, Worms was gradually rebuilt and in late 1699, he returned to Worms. This time he was appointed Rabbi! Alas, this was short lived, and he passed away on Rosh Chodesh Teves 1702.

Made in the USA
Columbia, SC
01 December 2024

2da2b9ad-c99c-4494-8f93-1cdaf2363adfR03